AMAZING WOMAN
DIVINE
LEGACY

A NEW ERA

Join the millions of women who are liberating
the wealth of feminine prosperity to reshape
their work, relationships, wellness and
ultimately the world.

Marsh Engle

©2024 Marsh Engle
Amazing Woman Divine Legacy
A New Era – Join the millions of women who are liberating the wealth of feminine prosperity to reshape their work, relationships, wellness and ultimately the world.

eBook ISBN: 978-1-962570-52-7
Paperback ISBN: 978-1-962570-53-4
Hardcover ISBN: 978-1-962570-55-8
Ingram Spark ISBN: 978-1-962570-54-1
Library of Congress Control Number: 2024903520

Cover Design by Marsh Engle
Interior Design by Marigold 2X
Published by Spotlight Publishing House –
https: SpotlightPublishingHouse.com

For More Information about Amazing Woman Nation go to:
www.AmazingWomanNation.com

AMAZING WOMAN
DIVINE
LEGACY

A NEW ERA

Join the millions of women who are liberating the wealth of feminine prosperity to reshape their work, relationships, wellness and ultimately the world.

Marsh Engle

Melissa Belongea, Sandra Girouard, Niloo Golshan,
Rocio Ortiz Luevano, Becky Norwood, Conni Ponturo,
CeCe Sanchez, Gina Shansey-Marder

Along with Influential Mentors, Entrepreneurs and Changemakers

SPOTLIGHT
PUBLISHING HOUSE
Goodyear, Arizona

Contents

*When a woman opens to the
radiance of her heart, all doubts
drop away and what remains is the
wealth of her divine legacy.*

Dedication

This book is dedicated to you,
a woman embracing the radiant wealth of her divine
legacy, shining light on the wisdom of her voice,
becoming a magnetic expression of feminine prosperity…
compassionate and intuitive…
innovative, collaborative, and encouraging…
heart-centered, receptive, welcoming…
joyful, trusting, inspired…
world-changing.

AMAZING WOMAN — It's a NEW ERA.

*Millions are answering the call to embrace
the wealth of feminine prosperity.
Because, Amazing Woman,
feminine prosperity is
the heart and soul of our Divine Legacy.*

Preface

More than a book, AMAZING WOMAN DIVINE LEGACY is a call for women to rise into a NEW ERA of liberating the wealth of feminine prosperity to reshape their work, relationships, wellness, and ultimately the world.

In a time when society often appears to value thinking over intuition; action over receptivity; and focusing our energy outward rather than inward — embracing the power of feminine prosperity is healing deeply rooted feminine wounds and their patterns of limiting perceptions, beliefs, and actions that come at a high cost of diminished purpose, confidence, well-being, success, happiness, and fulfillment.

Imagine those creative capacities you've yet to access...
the wisdom you've yet to give voice...
the passions you've yet to unleash.

To embody the essentials of feminine prosperity we must learn ways to embrace unconditional sacred confidence — we must devote the time to questioning, rebuking, reclaiming, and creating a shift in the retelling of our stories that have shaped our experiences — pausing along the way to assign a high value to the transformation that is being created.

It's an era of flourishing in an unshakeable feminine consciousness...
expressing the desires of our spiritual heart...
acting upon our highest intentions...
and realizing the most radiant of our potentials.

AMAZING WOMAN DIVINE LEGACY provides practical examples of feminine prosperity in action and gives you access to the most intimate of life-lessons and potent teachings from a collective of influential mentors, coaches, entrepreneurs, and impact makers.

Each of the co-authors and contributors shares stories of how they liberated their own feminine prosperity... overcame draining self-doubt, confusion, self-judgment, and discouragement... you'll read about how they found:

- Ways to create inner harmony... amplifying a balance between the wisdom of the heart and a stilling of the mind.
- Ways to set free the ability to rapidly transcend perceived limitations and diminished self-confidence.
- Ways to turn up the volume of their intuition... the sacred link to the true expressive genius of the heart.
- Ways to unlock the power to immediately shift their capacities to create and fuel their passion for making a difference in the world.

And you'll discover the key practices these acclaimed transformational authors use to elevate clarity, activate intention, take actions to shift out of a 'survival' mindset and set free a 'radiant' mindset essential to feminine prosperity.

- Learn what they did to turn heartbreaking setbacks and even debilitating losses into an elevated capacity to experience greater joy, creativity, passion, and expressive freedom in their work, relationships, and more.

- Learn how they moved beyond mis-aligned beliefs and paralyzing fear to engage the self-healing and self-love to discover and reveal their own divine legacy.

Most of all, every story you'll read here in the pages of DIVINE LEGACY reflects unconditional sacred confidence that's at the very foundation of feminine prosperity.

> *The power of our DIVINE LEGACY is expressed in not one way; but, rather in many shapes and forms... as founders, entrepreneurs, community leaders, CEO's — as mothers, teachers, innovators, healers — as career professionals, service providers, artists, authors, trailblazers, inspirers and more.*

It is important to consider that through the words, teachings, and inspiration carried on the pages of this book we are blazing a new trail of embodying our divine legacy. And as part of this trailblazing, we are collectively developing a new paradigm of *feminine prosperity*, one that encourages, collaborates, praises, values, and respects.

We are stretching the edges of what's been done before. Elevating a new way of seeing and trusting new possibilities. Causing real change isn't about living in the comfort of what's already been said and done. Rather, it's about shaking up definitions, breaking through boundaries. It's about evolving and disrupting the status quo. It's about allowing the true essence of our feminine consciousness to grow deep roots, shine light on higher potentials, and expand our presence in the world.

And as you reveal the radiance of your own divine legacy, you will no longer wait for success or a shift in circumstances to feel empowered or wait to reach a certain level of wealth to feel abundance. You'll remember the fullness of who you are. You'll remember forgotten abilities. You'll magnify your worth and manifest the unbridled expression of your soul's mission... elevating your abilities to define your life, your future, your destiny.

As we allow the unfoldment of
our divine legacy…
As we face the days ahead…
As we activate the power of our voices…
And welcome in a new era of
feminine prosperity…
We link arms and rise together.

Because that's the infinite power of feminine prosperity… that's the infinite power of the feminine heart… that, AMAZING WOMAN, is our Divine Legacy.

Marsh Engle

The Peacock

A sacred symbol of elegance, beauty,
spiritual awakening, wealth, and the divine feminine.

5 Sacred Meanings Associated with the Peacock

1. Beauty and Self-expression: The radiant display of the peacock's feathers represents beauty while its colorful display symbolizes self-expression.

2. Creativity and Life: The peacock feathers are often associated with the beauty of life, a passionate display of creativity and celebration.

3. Potent Energy: Peacocks are powerful creatures with potent energy and that, of course, includes their feathers.

4. New Beginnings and Potentials: The Peacock reminds of the power of being present to positive and new opportunities.

5. Spiritual Awakening: Possibly the most significant of all, the peacock is recognized as a symbol of transformation, renewal, and progress.

It's time to embrace our Divine Legacy,
the wealth of our feminine prosperity
infused with the power to transform our lives,
the lives of those around us, and even the world.

Introduction

I've got my hip thrust to one side; my cropped top yanked up leaving my soft belly proudly exposed. Across my face is a brilliant wide smile. And with an arm raised high in the air I'm holding a freshly caught fish. This is the uninhibited radiant creature I was before years of sexual abuse ravaged my spirit and I let fear seep deep into my bones creating a distance and a disconnect between my sense of safety in the world and the expression of my soul.

For years I held the image of this picture in my heart because it reminded me that there was a time when I lived unafraid, bold, safe in my body, safe in the world. I used this photo as a touchstone reminding me there was a time when a brilliant light easily streamed from my eyes… a light that I can only call unbridled wholeness… I was undivided… I was unashamed… and I was unafraid.

It wasn't until early mid-life that I began to heal.
And when I did, I immersed myself,
inhaling anything I could find about
the radiant expression of the divine feminine.

The first time I read the story of Japanese Sun Goddess Amaterasu I fell to my knees and sobbed.

This wouldn't be the last time I cried... I cried for the shame of the abuse I'd endured. I cried for the denial of my own worth. I cried for a longing to heal the divide between my spirit and my physical place in the world.

I cried. I cried for all the women who for whatever reason have found themselves engulfed in fear or self-doubt... those who feel unsafe being seen... all of the women who dim their light... all of the women who numb their emotions, deny their spiritual gifts, power through, silence their voices.

All the women who hide.

Amaterasu's story felt all too familiar.
Her story felt like my story.
But it also felt like the story of millions of women.

What struct me most about Amaterasu's story is the pivotal moment when she locked herself away in a cave... rolling a massive, heavy stone in front of the entrance... hiding away...hoping to ensure her light would ever be seen in the world, ever again...

Yes, her story felt all too familiar.

I imagined the possibilities, even the probability, of her silent suffering in isolation. Suffocating her significance. Denying her worth and diminishing her worthiness. Or, at least that's the way I felt as I hid my own light, silenced my own voice, struggled with honoring my own worth.

Then, one day I suddenly stopped crying.

And I became angry, quietly fuming inside.

No longer fighting with sadness and grief, I tried to understand how I could begin to heal the anger.

I sat in the anger. And sat even longer.

I sat long enough to see my perspective was shifting. And with that new perspective came a realization that changed my life, my work, and my presence in the world.

I realized I wasn't angry.
I was engulfed in terror, real paralyzing fear.

The trauma of feminine wounds had more than wreaked havoc on my relationship with trust and my sense of safety… I had come face to face with the wide, deep ravine that stood between my feminine spirit, my sense of worth, and my esteemed place in the world.

As we deepen into the richness of our stories…
healing ancient feminine wounds…
we open to the prosperity of our giftedness,
our infinite potentials, our intuitive expansiveness, our divinity.

Healing this divide would allow me to know the true wealth of feminine prosperity — it would allow me to break free from the patterns that drove and informed my way of thinking about myself and my potentials, shadowing the way I saw the world.

Healing this divide would set me free from toxic driving ambition and fling open the door to a kind of confident ease steeped in trust and spiritual purpose.

Healing this divide would halt the hustle and grind to achieve, the people pleasing, the chasing to prove myself worthy, the playing it safe, the over-giving and the undervaluing.

Healing this divide would begin to dissolve the barriers to a new relationship with sacred power — envisioning power anchored in a connection with my own divinity — keenly magnifying self-trust, self-belief — surrendering into a radiant embrace of the amazing woman I was called to be.

In essence, healing this divide would set free the spiritual confidence to accept, believe, and radiate a sense of personal authority that only comes from removing the lies I'd accepted as truth and knowing myself in unedited authenticity.

We are no longer willing to write ourselves
out of our own divine legacy.
We will no longer deny the divinity that reigns in our
worth, wholeness, brilliance, and purpose.

But most of all, I found that the healing of this divide had everything to do with liberating my voice and the voices of millions of women — igniting the willingness to stop looking 'out there' to fuel a sense of worth and worthiness — showing up for ourselves — moving our divinity out of the shadows and into the world.

The greatest source of the prosperity of any woman's life
lives in the voice of her soul.
And this is a voice only she can hear.

As she sets free the sacred confidence to hear this voice, she also sets free the voice of truth... the voice of love... the voice of intuitive guidance... she sets free her divinity, and this is indeed the sacredness of her life.

There are times we may feel as if we've
lost our way. But the divine within us is never really gone,
it's simply that our focus has been diffused.
So, if we find we've steered away from the
heart of our feminine prosperity,
we can remind ourselves the wealth of our divine legacy
can never be extinguished,
for it is, and always will be, speaking in and through us.

No doubt about it. It takes sheer devotion to change a story. We must invite in a deeper contemplation. And when we do, we will find it comes down to this one essential question:

Am I willing to love myself enough to be truthful and honest…
truly reach into the depths of my heart to feel and to realize
how gifted, powerful, and equipped I am?

The fact is the sacredness of our life is never far away. We cannot separate ourselves from our divinity. It can be hidden away. It can be buried in the deep crevasses of self-doubt and denial. But it is always there whispering the truth of our worth, calling us to share our love with the world.

And when we get still. When we listen closely. When we notice. We can see it reflected in the eyes of those who believe in us until we can believe in ourselves. We see it in those who rally around us, encourage us. We see it in a coming together over a common burning desire to rise in the wealth of our Divine Feminine, our legacy, the undeniable radiant wealth of our heart and our soul.

When a woman opens the radiance of her heart,
all doubts drop away and what remains is
the wealth of her divine legacy.

It is my prayer that within these pages you will find an unshakable bridge to make the shift into true sacred confidence and set free potentials you've yet to access… the wisdom you've yet to give voice… the passions you've yet to unleash.

At the heart and soul of feminine prosperity
is a mighty desire to create.
It's the call to become the amazing women we are called to be.

Acknowledging the qualities of feminine consciousness has been a running thread in human culture for thousands upon thousands of years — imbued into different mystical practices, both now and throughout history. Generally thought to represent the part of our consciousness that connects us to qualities like intuition, feeling, nurturing… the multifaceted qualities of feminine energy can't be represented by one single definition. Each generation must reinterpret it, redefine it, and find ways to embody it.

We can begin to reinterpret, redefine, and embody the qualities of feminine prosperity by exploring ways to empower, focus, strengthen, and amplify our energy, insight, and sheer presence. Here are a few ways I've pulled from my own spiritual practice. Each provides the structure to tap into feminine prosperity so we can experience even greater abundance, creativity, and passion.

TEN AMPLIFIERS OF FEMININE PROSPERITY

1. BREATH POWER INTO YOUR RADIANCE

Imagine with every breath you are deepening an understanding of your purpose, an acceptance of your divine legacy, bridging life and the radiant expression of your reason for being.

2. DIVINE INTUITION

Commit to activating a deep understanding of your emotions and allow your intuition to be the bridge to your divine self. Then, act from this place of knowing. This is the sheer power of feminine prosperity.

3. RADICAL RECEPTIVITY

Imagine yourself thriving with every new experience and each new idea, naturally drawing to you a stream of resources and opportunities. Stretch to allow a stream of receptivity to create a vibrant match between the essence of your energy and your infinite potential.

4. SPONTANEOUS CREATIVITY

Allow your soul to speak through your imagination... vision, dream, and invent. Commit to let go of the need to be perfect. Declare there is no 'right way' or 'wrong way' or the need to follow a particular set of rules. Create the space for the spontaneous fulfillment of your most heart-centered desires.

5. SACRED CONFIDENCE

True confidence isn't battling to overcome fear. Or the need to be fearless before you act. It's a call to magnify your relationship with trust... allow trust to naturally neutralize fear... allow trust to be your greatest ally as you step into the radiant wealth of your divine legacy.

6. LEAVE NO PART OF YOU BEHIND

As *psychologist* Carl Jung once said, "There is no light without shadow and no wholeness without imperfection." Embrace any lingering shadow agreements that stand between the freedom of your expression and the recognition of your infinite potentials. Shake up definitions. Break through boundaries. Evolve and disrupt status quo. Certainly, revealing shadow agreements can be a daunting task, but it can also be spiritually liberating. Accepting your shadow self is the only way you can ensure you leave no part of your brilliance behind.

7. SACRED SPACE

Dedicate a space where you can easily connect with your feminine prosperity. This is your space so fill it with what is meaningful to you — a single object such as a statue, sculpture, crystal or anything that symbolizes your commitment to yourself and inspires the stillness required to tune-in, elevate, evolve, learn, grow, and express.

8. PEACEFUL PRESENCE

Inner peace radiates outward. It is a soothing energy. It's an energy that exudes ease. At the core of a peaceful presence is a calm mind. It's this calmness that allows you to remain centered, grounded, and peacefully present even in the most stressful situations. Cultivate practices that create an inner environment where your peaceful presence flourishes. Then, allow this presence — this state of feminine prosperity — to walk into the world.

9. RADIATE MAGNETISM

Magnetism is a unique ability to tap into a radiance of energy, exuding confidence, and pure joy. It's an undeniable presence that draws people, opportunities, and resources. The power of magnetism is a feminine way of creating. So, let your passions shine through every aspect of your life simply by embodying more and more of your radiance-infused, heart-enlivened magnetism.

10. SACRED PAUSE

Practice a sacred pause, simply because it is always the perfect moment to amplify the wealth of your feminine prosperity. Begin by creating a habit of pausing and asking one question: *What is my body requiring now?* Maybe it is nourishment, a moment of stillness, some type of movement… the practice of a sacred pause is an energy activator that promises to increase your creativity, intuitive clarity, ease.

11. FORTIFY YOUR ENERGY

Rather than thinking of requiring a solid wall of boundaries to 'protect' your energy… consider a practice of fortifying your energy field. The easiest way to begin this is by acknowledging your worth and honoring your value. Discern investments of your energy and your attention. Magnify the choice of your actions. Be attentive to your words, the stories you tell, and the meaning you assign to them. To fortify your energy field is to amplify your feminine prosperity.

12. CREATIVE WELLNESS

Self-care is essential to your creative wellness – it is the fuel of your feminine prosperity. Prioritize healthy, natural food choices; daily movement; meditation practices; and self-care activities that feed your soul. Explore practices like breath-work, sacred dance, artistic expression, spiritual writing, and journaling.

NOW LET'S GET STARTED.

As you begin your journey through the stories shared in the pages of DIVINE LEGACY, the most important thing to remember is this is your own personal experience. The definition of what you consider to be feminine prosperity — or the ways you individualize or connect with your own divine legacy — is going to be different for everyone. It is a unique, individual path.

Here are five practices to support you in gaining greater value from your experience with this book:

Be willing to feel your feelings. Too often we expend enormous energy running away from or shielding ourselves from feeling — possibly because emotional connection has been misinterpreted as weak, purposeless, or diminishing.

To unlock our full creative wholeness we need to access, fully feel, and release emotion free of resistance and harsh judgment. Otherwise, the feelings we are denying become locked in our physical body, blocking the wealth of our creativity, wisdom voice, authentic expression.

As you begin to allow yourself to fully feel your feelings, the essential powers of feminine prosperity can flow freely. Remember, loving acceptance begins with self-acceptance. And it is self-acceptance that shines light on the essence of unbridled feminine prosperity.

Set aside sacred time. Gift yourself sacred time to experience the material in this book. Sacred time is defined as your willingness to give yourself the space to move through the stories at your own pace. This will also create the space for your intuition to speak and be heard. Imagine the impulse of your intuition as the voice of your feminine prosperity. And to fully access it, you must establish a sacred connection with your 'feeling body' devoting time for contemplation. Setting aside sacred time will allow you to define and/or redefine your relationship with your own divine legacy. Also, it will give you the time and space to discern the shifts you know are calling to you.

Dedicate yourself to trust. When your feminine prosperity begins to activate, awaken, and elevate, there will likely be feelings of heightened energy. Very often you will feel restless or find your mind spinning with thoughts or distracted by things you need to do. These are all signs new levels of feminine prosperity are being activated. Devote yourself to trust what you feel and any new insights that arise.

Cultivate stillness. Dedicating time to cultivating stillness and rest is vital for activating feminine prosperity. It is challenging to amplify your inner-awareness and move through necessary transformation if you are caught in a relentless cycle of rush, hurry, and hustle.

Cultivating stillness can become a regular practice; regularity over time fortifies and creates an inner environment steeped in connectedness, awareness, and strength... this not only amplifies feminine prosperity, but it magnifies the focused power of every action.

And one last thing before you begin...

The story of Sun Goddess Amaterasu continues...
as she sets free her innate feminine prosperity...
she moves the stone away from the cave...

she reflects her beauty…
she allows herself to be wholly seen…
she brings her light to the world …
and the world flourishes …
a NEW era of triumph feminine prosperity prevails.

As you take steps to move forward, it is important to consider, we are blazing a new trail of embodying our divine legacy. And as part of this trailblazing, we are collectively developing a new paradigm of feminine prosperity, one that encourages, collaborates, praises, values, and respects. One that celebrates, honors, and expresses our spiritual gifts.

Yes, we are stretching the edges of what's been done before. Elevating a new way of seeing new possibilities. And igniting infinite potentials.

As I've often said, causing real change isn't about living in the comfort of what's already been said and done. Rather, it's about shaking up definitions, breaking through boundaries. It's about elevating. And disrupting the status quo. And just as Sun Goddess Amaterasu reflected so beautifully… it about devoting ourselves to be wholly seen and our giftedness celebrated. It's about allowing our feminine prosperity to grow radiant roots and shine light on the world.

And that, amazing women, is something we do exceedingly well.

Marsh Engle

Today I cultivate a rich inner environment
of sacred confidence
so when I step into the world,
I am enlivened and equipped
to embrace my divine legacy.
I slow my spinning mind.
I become receptive to possibilities.
I take purposeful action.
Today I magnify the wealth
of my feminine prosperity.
My intention is clear.
My creativity fueled.
The esteem of my soul realized.

Amazing Woman Divine Legacy
The Sacred Agreements

As the Amazing Woman I AM, each moment I ignite a fresh new view of life and move beyond my set familiar ways. I recognize myself with mirror-like wisdom and set free the brilliance of my deepest heart's desire. I honor my creativity. I celebrate my beauty. I embrace my value.

As the Amazing Woman I AM, I open to a precious resource of guidance by becoming the observer of what life is always gifting. I choose to see things as they really are, let fresh insight easily arise and allow an even greater potential for life to emerge.

As the Amazing Woman I AM, I surrender into my Divinity and move into harmonious creative balance with life. Through clarity of intention, I open to and unite with the field of all possibilities. Infused with meaning and purpose, I AM inspired, empowered and free to innovate and realize the life I envision.

As the Amazing Woman I AM, I view life as a radiant romance with the new and unexplored. With ease and clarity of choice, I engage the balance of both giving and receiving. From this heart-centered connection, I allow a natural sense of passion and wonder to emerge.

With clear communication I set free an abundant flow of resources and prosperity.

As the Amazing Woman I AM, I know that an unbounded creative flow is set free as I allow myself to trust and act upon my intuitive callings. Poised in the confidence and faith of this assurance, I choose to relinquish all lingering attachment to self-doubt and fear. I now recognize that real power is accessed through a loving and trusting heart.

As the Amazing Woman, I AM, I know when I am true to myself, true to others and true to life, I live in the realm of feminine prosperity. Filled with a sense of direction and purpose, I unleash a limitless flow of joy and passion. Through this sense of pure devotion, I bring my highest expression of love to life.

Dedication

To all the resilient women of Iran and
all women refugees worldwide,
To the courageous souls on a quest for connection and belonging,
And to the remarkable women who have shaped my life
in my female lineage - my grandmothers, my mother,
my sister, my two daughters,
And to all my loyal friendships embodying
the true essence of sisterhood.

~Niloo Golshan

Chapter 1

Walking the Path of the Divine Feminine

Each of us experiences a transformative journey
of remembering ourselves...
calling back the fragmented parts of Self,
and integrating them into a deeper experience of
connection, authenticity, and wholeness.
I call this Walking the Path of the Divine Feminine.

Written by Niloo Golshan

I'm here to remind you, beloved sister that you too are Divine. You, too, are the Goddess merging with the Divine Feminine. I am here to help you remember your authenticity, your truth, your beauty, your love, your strength, your power, your grace, and all that you may have forgotten. As I did.

At the age of 18, I began my spiritual journey. I was searching for something outside of me to fill the void, to provide that sense of belonging, acceptance, and love. At that time, I didn't realize that I was embarking on a quest to find myself and I would never have imagined I would be writing these words to you today.

But truly I now see that at the age of 13 I was being guided into a transformation that would forever change my future and my deep connection with the Divine.

In 1978 at the tender young age of 13, riots broke out in Tehran, and my parents, seeking safety, planned what was meant to be a brief escape to Israel.

In the heart of Israel, as the realization dawned that we would never return to Iran, my world shifted tremendously. The upheaval started in Tehran, amidst the chaos and riots that transformed a supposed short vacation into a permanent exile. As weeks turned into months, the whispers of adults around me painted a grimmer picture. Iran was on the brink of a revolution; it was no longer safe to return. That was the moment my childhood innocence was shattered, replaced by the heavy mantle of adulthood. I was suddenly thrust into an abyss of uncertainty, grappling with the loss of my home, my friends, and all that was familiar.

The journey was far from over. After nine months in Israel, my family's path took us to New York and, eventually, to Los Angeles. Each relocation was a fresh start, a new battle against the tide of instability. In New York, I was a foreigner in a sea of unfamiliar faces, where my homeland was known only for its war-torn image, not for the rich culture and kindness that defined the true Iran.

The 1979 Iranian Revolution marked more than just political upheaval; it overshadowed the beauty and heritage of my homeland in the global eye. The world forgot the Iran of poetry, art, and warmth, focusing only on its struggles. With each move, I mourned not just the loss of my home but also the fading of a cultural identity rich in history and grace.

Yet in these times of change, and throughout my life, I found unexpected anchors — 'earth angels' in the form of friends who appeared when I needed them most, offering solace and connection. They stood as a testament to the divine's presence in my life, reassuring me that even as I navigated the loss of my homeland, I was still connected to something greater – a universal tapestry of human connection and resilience.

When I arrived in Los Angeles, I entered a world that was both familiar and alien. The city housed a large Persian community, many of whom, like my family, were refugees. Each person carried their own narrative of escape and loss, a mosaic of stories echoing my own. Yet, amid this shared backdrop, I found an unexpected disconnect. Despite being surrounded by those with similar origins, I felt an inexplicable distance, a gap between them and me.

Throughout the years, as I built connections and adapted to new environments, a profound truth remained hidden from my consciousness. It was four decades later that I came to realize I had inadvertently disconnected from the first 13 years of my life. This unintentional separation had created an invisible divide, separating my past from my present. I lived in a state of self-imposed exile. I had become numb to my country of origin and my culture.

As I navigated this path, I struggled with my identity. *"Who am I? What am I doing here? Where am I going?"* These questions continued to haunt me for years, and the urge to find a connection became an integral part of my journey.

Many masters and gurus, many teachings, many paths of discoveries have happened since I stepped on my spiritual path.

I prayed to the divine day after day, night after night. I was looking for direction, for clarity, for guidance in my life. And still I was anxious, depressed and felt totally lost! I was plagued by chronic illness, immense physical and emotional pain.

I found myself rushed to the hospital at 32, facing a week of uncertainty and fear, culminating in a diagnosis of Crohn's, an autoimmune disease. This was my body's way of signaling that something deeper was amiss.

Following my hospitalization, I embarked on a relentless quest for healing, feeling lonely and scared. I navigated a labyrinth of medical opinions, consulting various doctors and holistic practitioners, seeking any intervention that promised relief. This journey was more than just a search for a cure; it was a marathon of endurance, marked by an exhausting procession from one doctor to another, from one approach to the next, and a series of medications that seemed endless.

The driving force behind this exhaustive search was not solely my own well-being. It was fueled by a deeper, more compelling motivation – my two young daughters, aged two and seven at the time of my diagnosis. The love for my daughters became my beacon, guiding me through the fog of uncertainty and fatigue. I was propelled not just by the desire to be healthy for myself, but by the necessity to be strong for them. I needed to regain my health to take care of my daughters, to be there for their milestones, their joys, and their challenges.

In this odyssey of healing, I wasn't merely a patient seeking treatment; I was a mother fighting for the chance to be present in her children's lives. Every step I took, every new treatment I tried, was a testament to a mother's love and her unyielding spirit to overcome adversity for the sake of her children.

My healing process led me to understand that autoimmune disease is, in essence, the body attacking itself. This realization propelled me on a quest to understand why. I discovered that it was rooted in the trauma of losing my home, compounded by an unhappy and unhealthy marriage.

The only consistency in my life has been my devotion to my spiritual practice and my connection to the divine, and my faith in the universe.

In the darkest moments of my marriage, I found solace in an unexpected place: my closet. There, enveloped in darkness, I would close the door, sit on the floor, and let my tears flow freely. It became my sanctuary during times of turmoil in my marriage. My closet was my refuge, a place where I could cry and pray in peace.

During these moments of solitude and prayer, a recurring answer came from divine: *"You'll get a divorce."* This thought terrified me.

The idea of divorce was overwhelming, especially as a stay-at-home mother of two young children, grappling with illness without a job made the thought of leaving seem impossible.

The voice in my head, suggesting divorce, seemed absurd. *How could I, in my weakened state, consider such a monumental step?* I kept my marital problems a secret, confiding in no one. This secrecy, I later realized, was contributing to my health issues. The burden of keeping everything inside, managing my illness, caring for my children, and dealing with an unhealthy marriage, was immense.

I vividly recall this life changing morning about 15 years ago. While soaking in a Jacuzzi, nursing my aching body, a soft, gentle voice spoke to me: *"Dear Child, how can I continue guiding you if you ignore my messages?"* Later I realized it was the voice of the divine feminine guiding me.

Well, as you can imagine, that message shook me to my core! I knew that from that day on, I would have to listen to my inner Divine Feminine voice if I had any chance to evolve on my spiritual path.

I also knew that this would be an extremely challenging promise for a controlling perfectionist such as myself. Nevertheless, I chose to surrender to her, to truly listen, and that decision transformed my life.

I committed to a profound promise: to heed and act upon all divine guidance, not just the convenient parts. This vow steered me towards self-realization and embracing the Divine Feminine. Previously, my perception was filtered, tuned out to anything that might unsettle my seemingly perfect life. To the outside world, I appeared to have everything. Inwardly, however, I was emotionally fragmented, merely existing in a numb state of autopilot. Without realizing I was only acknowledging parts of divine wisdom that posed no threat to my life's superficial façade of a perfect and fulfilling life.

It was a desperate moment of clarity that jolted me into full awareness. I recognized that I needed to listen, for my own sake.

This realization sparked a devotion within me to reinvent myself, despite not knowing where to start or how to proceed. I found myself at a crossroads, facing the daunting task of dismantling the life I knew to uncover the authentic 'me' that had been buried under years of conformity and expectation. This process of awakening was not just about physical healing; it was a spiritual awakening.

I began to understand that listening
to the divine voice meant embracing change,
even if it meant stepping into the unknown.
It was about breaking free from the autopilot mode
that had kept me safe but unfulfilled and
venturing into uncharted territories of self-discovery and truth.

Embracing this journey was a testament to my strength and resilience. The path to rediscovery was fraught with challenges, but it was also filled with moments of profound insight and liberation.

What transpired then was the *"Dark Knight of the Soul"* where I got tested with much hardship and despair.

There comes a time when we must let go of old beliefs,
discard the masks we've worn that once served a purpose
but no longer align with our true selves.
These beliefs, doubts, and fears —
they whisper constantly in our minds,
pretending to keep us safe.
But in truth, they anchor us to past habits
and patterns that no longer serve our highest good.

I had this profound realization that came to me during my own journey of transformation. It was like undergoing a metamorphosis, a deep and personal change, and I feel it's important to convey this to you as you walk your path.

I've grappled with false voices in my mind – voices of doubt, fear, and outdated beliefs – all masquerading as protectors keeping me "safe." Yet, I realized that these false voices were chains holding me back, preventing me from surrendering to my highest self and moving forward in life.

This realization led me to what I can only describe as the death of my ego. It was a profound shedding of the various versions of myself that I had clung to, along with the beliefs that were never truly mine. This process was not gentle or easy. It demanded that I sit with myself, confront, and embrace every emotion that surfaced, without judgment or the urge to control.

I was guided to dive deep into the dark side of the Divine Feminine so that I can see my pain. Feel it fully, giving myself permission to let these emotions move through me. By facing and freeing emotions that had been trapped within me for so long, they transformed. They were no longer just pain or scars; they became lessons, purposes, guides to my next steps and finally leading me to the painful yet freeing decision of ending my marriage of 25 years.

This liberation was crucial. It meant I was no longer stuck in a loop of repeating the same old patterns. I was creating a new space within myself, a space where I could cultivate thoughts and beliefs that were authentic and true to me at that moment.

This encounter with the dark side of the Divine Feminine opened my eyes to the profound wounding of the divine feminine within my own culture, particularly as a woman from the Middle East.

I realized that the promise of healing wasn't just for me; it extended to my daughters as well, offering a chance to break the cycle of generational wounds and prevent their transmission to future generations.

There's a saying that resonates deeply with me:
'when one woman heals herself,
she also heals seven generations before and after her.'

Embracing this profound belief, I committed to my healing journey, a path that involved not only personal introspection but also a broader quest to restore the generational and ancestral traumas ingrained in my family's bloodline.

I realized that no one else could rescue me – it was a journey I had to undertake myself, with divine guidance. By choosing to listen and obey, even when it was challenging or didn't make sense, I began to heal.

I found myself, rediscovered my gifts, and learned to set healthy boundaries. I confronted my unhealthy relationships and took responsibility for my part in them.

Most importantly, I learned to love and accept myself completely.

My journey is a testament to the transformative power of the Divine Feminine. It's about finding your truth, stepping into the unknown, and surrendering to that inner whisper. It's a continuous spiral of evolution. It's a continuous process of death, rebirth, and metamorphosis where each step brings you closer to your authentic self.

This is my story, my path of becoming an iconic woman, walking hand in hand with the Divine Feminine.

Sharing this with you, I hope to convey that this journey of transformation is deeply personal yet universally relevant. It's about breaking free from the confines of our past selves and stepping boldly into a future where we live as our most authentic selves. This path I've walked is not just my story — it's a testament to the power of personal growth and the courage to embrace one's true self.

I want to share with you a meditation that has been a guiding light in my journey, and I believe it can illuminate yours as well.

This meditation can be practiced anytime, day or night. It's a powerful tool for grounding and connecting with Divine Guidance and Earth's nurturing energy.

To begin, close your eyes, whether you're sitting or standing. Take three deep breaths. Bring your awareness to your feet on the floor, feeling the solid Earth beneath you.

Acknowledge and thank Divine Earth for her gifts.

Ask her softly in your heart, *"Divine Earth, please ground me in your embrace, so that I am fully present in my body. Nourish me, so I may live vibrantly and fulfill my purpose."*

Continue with your breath and picture yourself as a majestic tree.

Imagine roots growing from your feet, delving deep into Earth.

Feel her nourishing energy coursing up your legs, revitalizing your entire being.

Now shift your focus to the top of your head.

Acknowledge the "Divine Presence" and her gifts. Request her guidance: *"Divine Presence, please fill me with your light of wisdom, guidance, and protection."*

Now visualize a beautiful, bright white light entering your body from above, filling every part of you with divine energy from head to toe.

Feel this light continuously integrating into every cell, vast and endless in its magnificence.

Sense this vibrant light energy overflowing from your body, extending around you like a sphere, creating a protective, radiant aura.

Now, gently place your left hand just below your navel, over the sacral chakra, a center associated with creativity, the emotional depth and the feminine.

Place your right hand over your heart center, the heart chakra which associated with love and compassion.

As the left hand is on the womb and the right hand is on the heart it creates a synergy.

Feel the heart and womb connection, the synergy of divine feminine and divine masculine energies within.

Embrace the sensations of lightness, joy, love, and protection emanating from this connection. Feel whole, filled with gratitude and abundance.

Take a deep breath and open your eyes.

Pause and ask yourself …

How does this meditation feel?

What sensations, energies or even messages are arising?

Each person's experience is unique, reflecting their divine blueprint.

Don't compare or judge your experiences; instead, cherish them.

Keeping a journal can help you remember and reflect on these moments.

When we awaken the Sacred Divine Feminine energy, we become present, empathetic, and deeply connected to others. We reawaken qualities of intuition, nurturing, creativity, emotional intelligence, and compassion.

As I have shared my experiences with you here, I have done so with an open heart. I hope that in reading my journey, you find the strength to confront your own fears, to embrace your own journey of self-discovery, and to recognize that in the tapestry of life, every thread, every color, every shade is vital to the complete picture. My journey of writing this chapter is a testament to the transformative power of listening to one's inner voice and the Divine, and the incredible growth that comes from stepping into the unknown.

I am an AMAZING WOMAN – AS YOU ARE.

About Niloo Golshan

Teacher, Mentor, Alchemist, and Sensory Transformation Facilitator

Niloo is a devoted Spiritual guide with over four decades of experience on a journey of self-realization and inner transformation. With a rare blend of empathy, a delightful sense of humor, and a talent for evoking joy, she creates spaces that awaken all five senses, inspiring a holistic approach to a healthy lifestyle. Niloo is a proud mother of 2 wise and well-rounded beautiful daughters.

Drawing from her personal journey through unimaginable hardships as a refugee, navigating challenging chronic health conditions, and a turbulent marriage, Niloo has undergone profound transformations in health, wealth, and personal relationships, shaping her into a compassionate and insightful mentor.

Since 2005, Niloo has been dedicated to teaching and guiding women inward, helping them rediscover their essence, truth, purpose, and inherent feminine strength. Through her commitment to creating beautiful and sacred rituals and spaces, she provides a nurturing environment where transformation can take place. Utilizing a wealth of experience in teaching Kundalini yoga and meditation, breathwork, Restorative yoga, women's healing circles, dance and movement, Bhakti yoga, and leading Kirtans, Niloo serves as a skilled healing practitioner, harnessing the power of the senses.

Niloo also offers compassionate guidance as a Death Doula supporting individuals and their loved ones through life's end, providing assistance in this deeply meaningful phase.

Her spiritual journey includes transformative pilgrimages to India and initiations into advanced Kriya meditations, immersion in the Sacred Geometry mystery school in Bali, as well as mystical initiations in the ancient goddess temples of Egypt.

With this rich tapestry of knowledge, wisdom and hands-on experience, Niloo is passionately committed to leading and supporting women on their paths of personal evolution and self-exploration. Niloo's dedication to the care of self and others inspires women to courageously reconnect with their body and spirit, re-claiming their power to speak up, to stand up for themselves, to show up, and to share their unique gifts with the world.

www.niloogolshan.com
contact@niloogolshan.com

Dedication

The words in this chapter are dedicated to my
Mom and Step-Mom.
Each has provided an example of spiritual practice
that has given me the same foundation.
And each has demonstrated love and compassion
in ways that are out of this world,
in ways that the world needs more than ever.
Their examples are lights that continue
to guide me along this path.

~Melissa Belongea

Chapter 2

Regenerative Relationships will Heal the Earth

Dream big. Cultivating the vision of your dream relationships and nurturing them in that direction every day is one of the most powerful things anyone can do to transform the mood of the world and the health of the Earth. Starting with self, then with others, and radiating out into the world, the quality of relationships at every level defines our collective human experience.

Written by Melissa Belongea

I found my way to my Air-bnb somewhere in Northwestern New Mexico. After settling in, I decided to go for a late evening drive when I made my way to the end of a dirt road. It was shaped like a horseshoe, ready to turn me back around from where I came. As I drove around the bend, resigned that I had reached the end, I looked out the passenger window to the North to see a field of obsidian formations.

I stopped the car; it was too beautiful to ignore. What was this place? A bed of volcanic activity in the middle of the desert. For miles, trails carved through peaks of smooth glass waves. Slowly I felt myself wake up. It was a dream. What did the sight of piled obsidian mean? It felt like a good omen. A harbinger of transitions. Deep in my bones, I feel a change coming. Obsidian has been associated with revealing hidden truths, knowledge, and insights. It is also known as a stone for healing, releasing blockages, transformation, and helping to initiate positive change. Somehow this dream felt like an invitation signaling that it is safe to enter a new space within myself and with others — a field of new possibilities.

Rarely have we been taught the art of loving ourselves as an intentional way of life, and when we are, we are taught that self-love is a solitary act.

Relationships are at the center of all creation; they define our entire existence. Starting with self, then with others, and radiating out into the world, the quality of relationships at every level of society defines our collective human experience. Yet, we so often forget that we are tied into a larger web of relating, even as the evidence is clear. We learn through our early experiences about how to relate to others.

Patterns found in adult relationships reveal what has been passed down from generation to generation until they are healed. Rarely have we been taught the art of loving ourselves as an intentional way of life, and when we are, we are taught that self-love is a solitary act. As interconnected people, our ability to love ourselves sets in motion a much larger ripple effect.

Because self-love ultimately impacts everyone we come in contact with, perhaps it helps to widen the definition. While love for self begins in our own private world, it is through interacting with others and our environment that we learn how to love ourselves more completely. It is through experiences with life that it returns us home to ourselves again and again.

Each time we may grow stronger in our connection to the mystery of it all, only to find that within our inner space is a portal to all creation. It is in this place, where we can deepen into stillness, that allows us to create a bridge of trust with the beautiful natural order that plays out behind the scenes of everyday life. The more time we spend refining our inner world, connecting intimately to ourselves, the more sensitive we become to the undeniable truth of our human nature: we are not separate from each other, but rather woven together in ways that perfectly support each other's growth as part of a larger design.

To be in love with oneself is to be in love with life.
In this way, perhaps the highest form of self-love is in relationships when
we can fully surrender our agendas and be in simple, full presence.

The beauty of spending time alone is that it requires us to become more loving with all of who we are. That's been my experience at least. For the last several years, as I've moved through various stages of nearly a decade of intense healing, I have found myself in a space of continual solitude. It has seemed as if no matter what I do to try and plug myself into a larger community, life has pointed me back to myself.

It's kind of like when I was a kid and not allowed to leave my room until it was clean. It's nature's way of telling me I've had more healing to do. Sometimes life will continue to carve out a path of solitude until you meet yourself with total compassion. Other times, once enough personal healing has taken place, greater healing can be done in relationships. Either way, in this fertile space we learn to accept our deepest flaws and greatest desires, forgiving ourselves for walking the path of being human and accepting ourselves as imperfect.

It is then that we enter a level of readiness to share life with others in a purer way where truly authentic connection is possible. To be in love with oneself is to be in love with life. In this way, perhaps the highest form of self-love is in relationships when we can fully surrender our agendas and be in simple, full presence — to be who we fully are. Perhaps self-love is being able to stand so whole in our own sovereignty that we are able to be there for someone when they need us most without losing ourselves. Perhaps self-love is being able to love all of humanity and the planet into greater wholeness, together.

To feel witnessed in the places I feel most broken
brings such a deep state of healing,
I can't help but wonder if self-love needs a reframe.

For me, no matter how much inner work I do, no matter how much healing, self-nurturing and care I cultivate within, I will still have places that are extra tender and need love. While it's primarily my responsibility to give that love to myself, relationships offer a tremendous chance to provide support in the spots where it's harder to do that for ourselves. To feel witnessed in the places I feel most broken brings such a deep state of healing, that I can't help but wonder if self-love needs a reframe. I know I would not have been able to find greater contentment within myself without the support and guidance of others. While no one can do for me what is ultimately my personal responsibility, it has been through the generosity of others' time, care, and wisdom that have graciously helped light the way toward better ways of being in relationship to myself.

I recently started participating in women's circles and have been amazed by the support they provide as a place to be seen, heard, and considered as an individual, something we don't always receive as women in society. It's been a deeply healing experience. These are sacred spaces where women can learn to let down their walls, see each other as collaborators, and construct more true experiences of themselves.

When women get together to intentionally support one another, the world shifts. Feminine energy contains both fire and water; at times burning down what no longer serves us, and at other times gently moving the flow of a river as we collectively shape the future of our planet.

How can we learn to hold others in a loving light despite their own blindness to their greatness until they can see it for themselves? As an act of self-love in itself.

As the world grows more complex, the ability to be connected in community is revealing itself as an essential survival skill. Within the system of patriarchy and the competitive culture it breeds, people are constantly bombarded with messages, both subtle and overt, of not being good enough or of being above or below others, reflective of its hierarchical thinking. It's not that it is impossible to cultivate self-love in this environment, it's that it takes incredible awareness and willpower to step out of unhealthy, enmeshed, or 'normal' ways of doing things in order to embody bold individuality.

As social beings, we are heavily influenced by social culture. I bristle every time I hear the sentiment, 'You can't expect anyone to love you when you don't love yourself.' Instead, I think, 'How can we learn to hold others in a loving light despite their own blindness to their greatness until they can see it for themselves?' As an act of self-love in itself. If relationships are a mirror, then by nurturing others with care and kindness, we nurture ourselves.

When we judge or push others away when our own feelings of unworthiness come up, we can choose to see it as a signal that greater self-love is needed. What if we stopped shaming each other for not knowing how to love ourselves when it's a skill that is rarely taught? What if instead, we made more effort to see each other in our imperfect humanity, and offer a kind gesture or word of encouragement, or treat everyone we cross with loving awareness, even in moments when it can feel the hardest? How might that shift the culture and reflect back to us the tenderness our hearts so often long for?

Since nothing is born out of anything other than love,
when we are connected in this way,
we are connected to the source of creation.
In other words, love is creation.

The power of intentional community is that we can learn how to balance our relationships with ourselves, each other, and ultimately the Earth. There is a concept in geometry called a 'fractal', which is a never-ending pattern. Fractals represent individual parts within a greater ecosystem and provide a model of how humans can relate to each other and their environment. By focusing on and tending to the micro-universe of our immediate space, we are also impacting the larger energy body of our planet.

Fractals help us understand that by mastering love at the individual level, we can magnify that effect at the global level. Love is a mysterious field, yet it is the most tangible, logical, resilient force in existence. It's the only force that can heal. By connecting to our own inner sense of self-love, we begin to feel this presence grow in greater and greater ways. Since nothing is born out of anything other than love, when we are connected in this way, we are connected to the source of creation. In other words, love is creation.

Lately, I have felt my own field of energy consciousness shifting into what I can only describe as a greater state of awareness of the subtleties of my environment and the feeling of cohesion between mind, body, and heart. Some call this 'flow state' and it opens up once we find our way into a more concentrated stream of loving awareness. There are many ways to get there, including spending time in nature, creating art, movement and exercise, eating nourishing foods, and taking time to be in stillness, whether gazing at a sunset, reading something meaningful, or simply finding quietness throughout the day. With this shift has been a greater connection to my spiritual gifts. I believe we all have these gifts, and that it is a matter of IF we choose to open up to them in a world that tells us that to be spiritual is to be 'weird'. Spirit is the most natural state there is, as it describes pure essence. What is the essence of you, animals, a tree, or anything? When we tune into that level of awareness, no longer do we see people for who they are on the surface, but we can see them in their full being.

With enough people focused on expanding their own state of self-awareness, sensitivity, and empathy, these forces can only grow.

As a highly sensitive person or empath, I've always been in tune with my environment on a deeper level. I relate to the world through underlying energy patterns and have a clear sense of knowing (Clair cognizance) and a clear sense of feeling (clairsentience). Others might have senses like clear sight (clairvoyance) or clear hearing (clairaudience). If all of this sounds unrelatable, consider the last time you had a feeling in your gut about a certain outcome, or thought of someone, only to hear from them or run into them out of the blue.

The more time people spend tuning into their own sensitivity, the stronger intuition grows and the more commonplace these coincidences become. It's taken a long time for me to fully step into this truth and say out loud that this is how I move about in the world, but after years of developing my sensitivities, these abilities are only getting stronger and I'm finding they are making life richer. Instead of hiding them away, I am grateful for them and want to use them to express greater clarity, creativity, and to experience the directness that life has to offer by being ever more present to my surroundings.

With enough people focused on expanding their own state of self-awareness, sensitivity, and empathy, these forces can only grow. In a world with so much strife, the medicine of self and shared love is our most abundant resource. Thinking back to the fields of black obsidian, I haven't had such a vivid dream like that in a while. It filled me with happiness, awe, and grounding. Sometimes I wonder if dreams are a way we communicate with nature and remember our future. Either way, I am content knowing that at least for me, it felt like a clear opening to a new reality that I am just starting to experience — a bridge to learning how to love in a new way. How do we as humans heal the many divides between us? How can we take our relationships to the next level and move past hurtful cycles and into a state of widespread abundance?

With all that we face in terms of climate change, social conflict, mental health challenges, changes in technology, and the shifting of resources on our shared planet, the future is no longer out in the distance — it's here, today, requiring that people come together in totally new ways. In order to get to the next phase in humanity, relationship structures will be required to move from extractive to regenerative, from linear (goal-oriented) to non-linear (process-oriented).

After studying human and relationship culture over the past twenty years and seeing the need for people to develop greater emotional and intimacy skills in all areas of life, I've consolidated the main themes I've observed into a single, four-part framework called: The Regenerative Relationship Method. Because I wanted people to have an accessible tool, I created it to apply to any relationship setting. My belief is that by having clear phases to work through, people can more easily transform the culture of relationships together.

By setting an intention to improve the quality of relationship culture, we can focus our attention and find common ground with others who are invested in the same outcome.

The Regenerative Relationship Method is a principles-first guide to creating a regenerative future, a simple method for working on relationship skills in the midst of everyday life in order to improve the quality of human culture. It all starts with intention, as the first and primary principle. By setting an intention to improve the quality of relationship culture, we can focus our attention and find common ground with others who are invested in the same outcome. Gathering around a shared intention includes the ability to be curious, maintain humility, and a sense of humor in the face of different perspectives.

The second principle is integrity. This means committing to finding alignment with others and creating harmony in a way that is rooted in honesty. Sometimes people may find themselves on the same wavelength naturally. Other times it takes effort to reach a place where people can understand each other in their authenticity. Vulnerability, self-responsibility, and intimacy all contribute to maintaining integrity in our relationships. Once an intention for relating has been set and integrity is established, trust begins to take root. This is the third principle.

Through enduring trust, there are no obstacles that can't be overcome. Trust can be further animated through abundance, collaboration, and pollination. Abundance is marked by trusting life to unfold naturally and can apply to a conversation, a situation, or the dissolving of a destructive habit. We are constantly evolving, and trust allows us to surrender to the ever-unfolding nature of our experiences while being present in them. Trust is also the foundation of all good collaborations, where psychological safety exists, leading to a greater pollination of ideas.

When we align our relationships to cycles found in nature,
instead of resisting life, which only causes suffering, we can affirm it.

Finally, the last principle is expansion. This is when a relationship has been through the stages of intention, integrity, and trust and is grounded in enough safety to allow for expansion into new levels of awareness. Expansion is marked by the qualities of leap, transcend, and begin. Once safety is established, larger risks can be taken leading to quantum or subtle leaps that allow people to transcend to a new level of awareness and relating. It is at this point that we are back to the beginning, ready to start the process all over again. The Regenerative Relationship Method mirrors the cycles of seed, life, death, rebirth. By syncing our relationships to the ways nature works, we discover a much greater power to support a healthy structure both personally and globally. When we align our relationships to cycles found in nature, instead of resisting life, which only causes suffering, we can affirm it. It is here that we can begin to find a balance between extremes (left vs right, capitalism vs socialism, male vs female, etc.) in order to celebrate the whole of humanity and our place in nature.

During a time of immense transition on the planet,
creating harmony with each other is one of the most impactful
things we can do to forge a healthy future.

As more people seek ways to improve their relationships with themselves, at home, in business, and out in the world—tools like The Regenerative Relationship Method can help speed up the process as we face more challenging global situations. During a time of immense transition on the planet, creating harmony with each other is one of the most impactful things we can do to forge a healthy future. Starting small, in your immediate universe of people makes the work approachable and easy to see immediate impacts.

My deepest hope is that more people realize the rewards of this challenging and ultimately fulfilling work in order to reach the abundant harvest on the other side of healing our relationships, and in turn, our world. It may sound wild to dream that big, but with a clear intention and commitment, anything is possible. Nature works in predictable ways; it is always striving for balance. The sooner humans align with this truth, the easier it will be for us to find balance as well.

One way to get started is to spend more time in nature observing the ways she moves, absorbing her moods, and appreciating the vastness she provides for all of life. Earth is quite literally our Mother. Connecting to the source of creation helps connect us back to ourselves and to the beauty of feminine energy in all of us. From here, consider what you dream for your own relationships.

Dream big. Cultivate the vision and then spend time every day choosing to nurture your relationships in that direction because at the end of the day, relationships are the center of life and the source of all creation. In Harvard's longest running study on happiness, it revealed that the number one predictor of health is close intimate relationships. This means creating a culture of regenerative relationships is one of the most powerful things anyone can do to transform the mood of the world and the health of the Earth.

About Melissa Belongea

Melissa Belongea is a writer and creative strategist serving individuals, entrepreneurs, and company leaders who desire breakthroughs in creating conscious lives, starting with relationships. Using The Regenerative Relationship Method, Melissa guides people to draw from the wisdom of natural cycles to uncover and align with their most authentic expression. Being truly seen and heard in all areas of life is a courageous act that begins with intention and a strong relationship with self.

Each time we peel back another layer to reveal more of our authenticity, first with ourselves and then with others, we step into a powerful space of creation and confidence. The world needs people who are brave enough to shed external expectations and create lives of vulnerability, connection, and intimacy—the stuff of authenticity.

Melissa brings together a powerful combination of broad (yet nuanced) cultural study, a professional background in creative strategy, and intuitive energy awareness to help her clients clear blocks and locate areas of greatest impact in their personal and professional lives.

Helping people define, refine, and express their purpose out in the world is at the core of this work, since misalignment of any kind is often rooted at the spiritual or energetic level. The Regenerative Relationship Method helps connect people to their unique authentic path by improving their relationships with themselves, others, their work, and their legacy or lasting impact.

For more information about Melissa Belongea and her work visit:
www.dmcostudioca.com or
www.melissabelongea.com or
@dmco.studio

Dedication

I dedicate this chapter to the women who
rise from the ashes, time and time again.
To the resilience of the human spirit that
thrives on love, faith and kindness.
To the dreamers who
dare to envision a better life and world,
and to the obstacles that ignited the phoenix within.

~Gina Shansey-Marder

Chapter 3

Adventures in Forgiveness

Self-Forgiveness is the ultimate level of forgiveness.
It opens the pathway to self-love...
the authentic light that leads to
living our heart and soul's deepest passions
and manifesting our greatest visions.

Written by Gina Shansey-Marder

The human experience is all about change. Nothing ever stays the same. *Wouldn't life get boring with things always being the same?* My story isn't about one experience that transformed my life, but about hundreds and thousands of experiences that have transformed me and my sense of being in this world. Some were grand experiences, and some were so small and yet, so incredibly powerful. As it is said, *"the teacher appears when the student is ready."* The beautiful part is, we will continue to transform for eternity. The goal is not the destination but the journey getting there.

Accountability or victim loop – Which one will you choose?
What we create on the inside, we create on the outside.

I believe each one of us has something we would benefit from by healing. We've all been pained somehow and in some way. *Who hasn't suffered from a broken heart... the loss of a loved one... or, by any other hurtful experience that people all over the world go through every day?* We all have pain. *But have we stopped to see on a deeper level how WE may, at times, be responsible for our own suffering? Does the quote "It's not the hand you were dealt, but the way you play your cards." get you thinking?* Or the rubber band example. The farther the rubber band is stretched back, the faster and further it will shoot forward. I believe that the farther we may be pulled into the darkness, the faster and further we will shoot into the light. If we remember, life is 10 percent what happens to us and 90 percent how we react to it.

I was born in Hollywood California to a 20-year-old mother who was heavily addicted to heroin and married to my father who she met while bartending at a local strip club. When I was 18 months old my mother was put in prison and my father split town, so I was taken in by my grandmother who eventually arranged for my uncle and his family to gain legal custody of me. My childhood memories are filled with lies, fear, abandonment, and psychological and physical abuse, at the hand of my aunt Vivian who I was led to believe was my mommy. But somehow, I was a happy kid most of the time. At least when I wasn't being the focus of Vivian's rants, humiliation, and rage. Eventually things got completely mental with this family, and I was 100% living on my own from the age of 14 1/2. I never saw what I had known as my mother, father, sister and two brothers, ever again. Even to this day.

Chapter 2 of life begins. Who am I?

Overnight I was sent to Hawaii to live with my grandma who had just been diagnosed with cancer. I was her caregiver from the moment I arrived. After a year of treatment my grandma was doing better and was able to care for herself a bit again. During this time, I was able to get out and live a little and quickly fell in love with a man 8 years my senior. We moved to London and got married. I was only 16 then, and I was the teen girl with big daddy issues. I left everything and everyone I knew, and I took a leap of faith, but I was too young and naive and soon found myself pregnant twice and in an abusive relationship. After two heart scaring abortions we moved back to Hawaii. I was happy to be back in Hawaii taking care of my grandma and spending quality time with her. But my heart continued to ache at the thought of my lost children. And as the months flew by my grandma's health began to decline and soon, she took her final breath and went home. That was the end of family love as I knew it. Soon after, my marriage fell apart, and my husband and I quickly went our separate ways. I was drowning in heartbreak.

Life became extremely challenging at that point. I really had no one and no support. And my birth mother was living on the same island at that point. I was always so hurt that, after she got out of prison both times, my mom just went about her life and never came to rescue me. So, I didn't expect anything from her at that time, even though she was finally sober and eventually became an addiction counselor and stayed sober for many years. But sadly, in the last few years of her life she began using again. The family was devastated and scared for her and our family's future. Especially because this time her drug of choice was meth, a very scary drug that was plaguing the area at the time.

It was soon after I lost my grandmother, my life slipped into an array of experiences that involved homelessness, hunger, rape and so much fear. I turned to the local punk rock street kids, music, alcohol, and drugs to find a family, freedom and happiness. And at times, I really found it!

At 19 I moved to California and the process of growing up began. Over the years I cleaned up my act, stopped drinking and drugging and started spending all my time reading every book I could find on spirituality and quantum physics. I practiced mindfulness, meditation, and yoga. I attended many healing retreats and utilized every tool I could get my hands on to figure out who I was, what I wanted in life and what life meant to me, on my terms! I was single at this point, intentionally. It was time to do me.

Life got wonderful. I had a great apartment near the beach in Santa Monica, a great job making great money and a tribe of sister friends that I still have to this day. Healing my hurt, exploring my learned belief systems, and creating my own belief systems and exploring this gorgeous planet became my reality. I had come so far, and I was proud of myself. I reconciled my relationship with my mother and two little sisters. I finally had a family again! And what could be greater? It was my real family.

Dancing my way into CHAPTER 3 of my life – I like who I'm becoming!

One of my lifelong dreams was to start a band. And it came true. Becoming one of the most wonderful experiences of my life. Connecting and creating with other artists is a soulful deep experience. We had a blast! We wrote and recorded a ton of original songs and performed for several years all over Southern California. I started to see and understand manifestation on a deeper level at this time. I was experiencing my dreams turning into reality right before my eyes and thankfully I didn't just chalk it up to *"it is what it is"*, I took notice. I was realizing by seeking my truth, healing my wounds, letting go, and growing and taking responsibility of myself and my life, I was opening the channels to allow my dreams to manifest.

There were so many teachers to explore. I was so passionate about soaking it all up, trying it all out and finding what resonated with my heart and soul. And I did. What a gift and blessing!

I was 29 now and life was so magical at this point. I had a good relationship with myself. I was on the top of the world and living my dream life. Then suddenly one of the biggest traumas of my life arrived. I was on my way home from a recording session, and I remember thinking how I couldn't wait to let my mom hear these songs and how she was going to love them. Even though she was addicted to drugs again, I was still very close and nurturing with her. At times I felt like I was her mother. I eventually arrived home, greeted my cats, and proceeded to check my answering machine. This was before cell phones btw. I looked at my phone and saw that I had 17 messages. That was unusual. I pressed play and there began the unfolding of message after message from different family members and friends. The panic and broken voices unveiled the darkness of my new reality. The messages started with, *"Gina, where is your mom? Your guy's house is on fire. Your mom's car and purse are there but we can't find her"*, and they ended with, *"your mom has been in a terrible fire, she has finally been found but she is burned extremely bad and is at the Loma Linda burn ward."*

I made the 2-hour drive to my mother and family in complete shock and deep devastation, confusion, and fear. We lost her the next day. And the reality was that my mother burned in an explosion caused by cooking meth in our garage. My reality broke into a million pieces.

For weeks I was in a daze and barely functioning. Eventually I knew I had to figure out how to get through this unending pain and confusion. I had to muscle up and dive deep within and make sense of what I was feeling, or else God only knows what else I would have done. Thankfully at the time I was reading the book and practicing the exercises in the *"The Artists Way"* by Julia Cameron. One of the practices is called *Morning Pages*, which is a form of release work and free form journaling that you commit to do each morning. Sometime after my mother's passing, through my journaling I was directed to write my mother a letter.

During this experience I began to see her through a different lens, with a new perspective and brighter light. I imagined her as a little girl, an individual, as a woman and a human being with a soul. I tried to see and understand her life and all the disappointing and terrible experiences she had been through. I wasn't excusing her choices and actions, but it made it much easier to understand. I realized that it wasn't about me and that I wasn't going to take it personal. And this is where I was taught the clearest lesson of forgiving others. We can't hurt another without hurting ourselves.

> *"The wound is the place where the light enters you."*
> *– Rumi*

Free falling into CHAPTER 4 of my life – WTF REALLY???

As life moved on, I revived myself once again and began the climb back up that steep hill to living a balanced and happy life. I continued learning, seeking, and growing. Eventually I remarried and began my career in women's health and wellness. Again, I was back connecting with my intuition and manifesting the life I wanted. I had a great 17 years of success in my industry and a good marriage. Then simultaneously both of those areas of my life crumbled and ended just as I was diagnosed with stage 4 cancer at 47. WTF! And the next life challenge began! Nowadays I call them lessons of love. This one took me even deeper than the last, but at this point in life I was way too tenacious to lose or give up! I decided I was going to win this battle even though the expressions on the faces of those closest to me were telling me otherwise.

Soon after my diagnosis a professional colleague and friend who had known about the current state of my health, dreadful divorce, and my departure from the company I had been an vital part of developing for 15 years, kindly overnight mailed me a book by Louise Hays called *You Can Heal Your own Body*. I read the whole book that night and became aware that I had created my own Dis-Ease! I had got caught up in life and career and began carrying around irritations, resentments and exchanging with other negative energies. I may have learned to forgive others, but I now realized I needed a reboot. *And how could I forgive myself for this?* I lost my breath initially then I decided to just roll my sleeves up and I said, *let's do this!*

I started with shadow work and going deep within to find the patterns that my life pains had left me with. I celebrated the gift of emotion and the ability to feel all of it. Joy, excitement, love, and even fear, sadness, and grief. There is something beautiful and healing happening when we allow all our emotions the freedom to be an equal part of our experiences. We have been taught to view sadness and grief as negative, but we each have the personal power to shift that belief and honor all our emotions. Next step was self-love. *I love myself, don't I?* And down the rabbit hole I went trying to understand how to really, really love myself. I learned that happiness was an inside job, and I began the process of reparenting myself. Reparenting is one of the deepest levels of self-love. We can give ourselves the understanding, safety, love and support we didn't get from our parents.

I could look at my life as a stream of bad luck, even a curse even. I chose differently. At this point in my life, I had been working so hard on trying to heal myself on multiple levels from all the different traumas, however I began to understand that while forgiving others was a beautiful intention, it was basically meaningless without learning to forgive myself first. I was determined to find a way to let go of what I once perceived as pain and hurt from family members, love relationships, colleagues, and friends. But the biggest one was with me! To forgive myself in every way, which there were so many layers of it I needed to work through.

Forgiving myself for not setting clear boundaries, allowing myself to take things personally, reacting in ways of fear, anger and resentment which do not serve me or the collective, for self-sabotage and so much more. It takes a real deep effort of self-awareness to find your truth. I called upon all my spiritual tools to support me through this process. The lessons I had attained over the years helped guide me to seeing myself for who I truly was deep inside, which led me to the first steps in connecting with true self love. I needed to release the limiting beliefs I had about myself and the world around me. I went deep and loved on myself hard. Everything I wished I was told and given as a youngster I now gave and said to myself, and it felt beautiful.

> *The longer you dwell in it, angel, the longer you dwell*
> *in it... remember you are free to choose but you are*
> *not free of the consequences of your choices.*

37

Facing my fears in CHAPTER 5 of life – Life is an adventure in forgiveness...

I recently was at a healing resort in Mexico that offered daily mind and body workshops as well as ancient rituals ranging from yoga and meditation to gratitude and transmutation rituals, forgiveness, and fire ceremonies. My husband and I attended so many of these workshops and had some very transformative experiences. One that really gave me a deep sense of healing was the forgiveness ceremony. We arrived at this beautiful studio right where the jungle meets the sand and sea. It was authentically calming there.

The forgiveness facilitator was a beautiful Brazilian woman who led us into a meditation. She then asked us to call into our imagination someone we want to forgive us or who we want to forgive. She then mentioned that it didn't have to be one person, it could be a group of people. I began calling in a group mixed with family and loved ones and myself. As she guided us through this process, I became an emotional hot wreck! Tears were just flowing out of me like a tropical storm as I lay there on the floor of this studio with a bunch of strangers who were seeking forgiveness of their own. It was a beautifully painful process until the moment she said, *"Now I want you to thank those who you need to forgive, for being your teachers."* Wow!! My teachers?? The emotional and physical abuse, the abandonment? Oh wait, YES! YES! YES!

All the traumatic experiences and great experiences had made me who I am, and I loved who I am. Just that paradigm shift in my perspective was so powerful and really gave me a sense of accountability. Because yes, my soul chose these experiences, energies, and brought people into my existence to learn and grow my spirit to the highest good for myself and for the collective.

Through each of my life journey experience's, the good and the bad, I've come to understand that we share this planet with people of many different levels of consciousness and no matter the level each person is at, God/Source loves us each equally and we are all equal in the eyes of God. Some are more elevated in their understanding, and some are figuring it out. Every soul has the free will and must go through their own journey, and they can't skip any stages. This is why it is so helpful to remember to never take things personally. When you feel as if someone said or did something to hurt you, it is always about them, not you.

A big lesson for me on my journey was that by forgiving and letting go, I could understand and see that we are all here exploring and making mistakes, and those mistakes are our teachers.

We each have the power to manifest any life we desire... to feel anyway we desire... and let go of all that doesn't serve us... we can heal the grief, trauma, fear, and pain while finding our way to self-realization and self-love. We can begin to understand the laws of the universe and the magical powers we each possess. It starts with stopping the blaming of others and owning our own life and experiences. Taking the high road and choosing to go within to love yourself and celebrate our uniqueness. And because happiness is an inside job, we need to stop looking for other people, places, or things to define our happiness and inner peace. We are all one energy, frequency, and a part of source, experiencing a life in the dimension of our choosing. Whether we choose to vibrate at a high or low frequency, our energy travels outwards to the collective energy field. We each chose to come here to learn and to grow our consciousness.

You can generate a positive outcome no matter how negative or difficult a situation may look from the outside. There are incredible levels of happiness, wellbeing, and inspiration that we all can experience here on earth when you are willing to follow your passions and actively create the life of your dreams.

"Forgiveness is not an occasional act; it is a constant attitude."
– Dr. Martin Luther King Jr

Soaring into the now of my life — Dreams realized and wishes granted!

One of the hardest things to do is to move forward without having all the answers. Sometimes we need to move on not exactly knowing why and be ok with that. Closure is really all about us. We chose to put one foot in front of the other each day, no one can do that for us.

I am no longer the person I used to be and that is called Evolution. I understand that we all choose the frequency that we want to vibrate at. That is free will. Through self-refection and examination with the exploration of physics, quantum physics, psychology, science, and spirituality I can now see how Iconic my life is, as each of our lives truly are. What a beautiful journey and gift each moment of life is. It all makes sense to me now. The dark and the light. The good and the bad.

This life and world are our incredibly magical playgrounds and once we figure out how to navigate our lives by finding inner peace through self-awareness, letting go of what isn't serving us any longer, being present and showering ourselves with pure unconditional self-love, it is then that we can begin the beautiful and ecstatic dance of life we each 100% deserve. We need to stop taking it all so seriously. We came here to have fun and live our best lives! Our world is currently at a place where all the information, knowledge, and data on how our world and Universe work is at our fingertips. So, if we chose to remain in our cluelessness and refuse to redesign our belief systems, then the path most likely will be layered with resistance. I suggest coasting down the path of least resistance and owning your incredible innate power.

Today I am friends with my ego. I understand that my ego is not who I am, and I have lovingly trained my ego to serve me to reach for my highest good and to never distinguish itself as separate from anyone or anything. The idea of death of ego, I believe, isn't self-serving. Our egos are a gift when we learn how to manage this aspect of our existence. I've earned my pure and bona fide self-esteem and self-importance through an unshakeable acceptance of all that is, all that I am and with a daily authentic practice of self-love and care.

To pursue purpose, you have to heal. I have now reached a state of consciousness where I am able to positively influence my surroundings. By choosing every day to vibrate at the highest frequency I am capable of… and calling upon my tools of intuition, manifestation, meditation, journaling/writing, body movement, breathwork and visualization… by taking initiative with mindfulness and equanimity… I allow myself to experience the blessings and majesty that is always surrounding me, in every way. It allows me to have a clear view of the actual lightness of it all and even the innate humor weaved deep within. The things that once annoyed me now give me a good chuckle.

As my words and thoughts are the seeds to the harvest of my future, today I choose, in my consciousness, to be devoted to Source, Love, Growth, Goodness, and Service.

Namaste

So, today as I write this message to you, I ask myself: *What does it mean to live an iconic life? To be an Iconic person?*

Does it mean being the most successful entrepreneur, sports hero, doctor, or rock star?

I believe being Iconic means living an aligned life with yourself and all of the energies and aura's we are coexisting amongst. To be excited by the notion of continuously being a seeker of enlightenment, growth and spiritual self-discovery while sharing your wisdom and being in service to the matters you feel a deep passion for. Those passions that bring light, love and understanding to you, the world and all the souls we share this experience with.

"Your thoughts create your reality. Manifest that sh*t!"

We've all heard phrases of this nature hundreds of times, but how do we do it? How do we apply these techniques and principles into our lives? It sounds so simple, right? And then we try but fail, which causes us to question the power of our thoughts. Or the idea that manifesting is even real. Next, if we are paying close attention, we become aware that our thoughts are in control of us rather than us in control of our thoughts. Understandably! We arrived at this life and world with complete amnesia. We have forgotten who we really are and what incredible powers we each possess. We've forgotten what we truly signed up for and what we came here to experience and learn.

We are born into the lives of the other human souls who are trying to figure out who they are and what it is they are here to do. And each of us learns about the world and life, initially through the lens of our parents, family, places of worship and our communities. Those perceptions can easily become our own. And this is where the Ego is born. Ego — a person's sense of self-esteem or self-importance.

The ego distinguishes itself as separate from the self of others.

"It is better to light one small candle than to curse the darkness."
—Eleanor Roosevelt

This journey we signed up for can be a tough one. Luckily, we have always had the ability to make our own choices. And sometimes… many times… it can be a long road until we "remember" this amazing gift of ours. And this, my amazing woman friend, this is where mindfulness becomes our very best, most meaningful mentor.

About Gina-Shansey-Marder

Gina Shansey-Marder is a lover, artist, published author, animal rights activist, tree hugger and survivor. She is passionate about nutrition, emotional and physical wellness, and is a spiritual growth enthusiast. For over 24 years her relentless passion has been anchored in coaching women of all ages and cultures.

Gina's mission is to guide and support women in discovering healing from painful life experiences and trauma so they can live their absolute best lives. Through shared lessons of the heart, deep understanding and compassion and the secrets of our Universal powers and gifts, it is Gina's goal to give women the tools, confidence and power to heal themselves and to fall in love with themselves, their unique talents and passions and their amazing lives.

She is currently devoting her time as a mentor, sound healer, published writer, singer/chanter, spiritual retreat designer and creator, meditation guide and owner and facilitator of Heaven's Hill Estate and Spiritual Retreat Sanctuary.

For more information on Gina, wine or retreats please visit www.heavenshillestate.com

Dedication

I dedicate my chapter to all the unsung songs yet unwritten.
To all the paintings yet painted. To all the poems yet heard.
To all the artists beaming with ideas. To all the artistry vision-inspired.

To reset and rise. To the birth of an artist. For the beginnings.
For being prolific. And for being still to listen to the wind.

The way of the artistry of alchemy, a path to the embodied authentic intuitive
self. She who weaves the unseen to seeing.
By a creative journey of courage. An awakening to creative trailblazing.
She who writes emerges from the depths of her soul.
She who dances through fear.

I dedicate this chapter to all the women who have dreamt of being.
The time is now to live it. Thank you, great spirit. Thank you, Creator.

I want to thank my ancestors, mentors/teachers and their teachers/teachers.
And to all the mystics I have met along the way.
She who is vulnerable to expressing herself creatively.

To all the strong women in my life. She who is powerful!
To my grandmothers, my mother. To my daughter.

To my granddaughter, and her granddaughter's granddaughter
To nature, where I find inspiration and restoration.
And mainly to Gaia. She who is mama, heart, home, stars
and moon and beyond the infinite Cosmos.

~CeCe Sanchez

Activate Your Inner Artist of Alchemy, the Creative Heart of Your Most Authentic Self

*The way of the alchemist symbolizes creative transformation
through the growth of authentic expression.
She successfully expresses herself through Love.
She honors the power of quietude over the
noise and chaos of a distracted mind.
She knows her power and freely expresses it.*

Written by CeCe Sanchez

Why is it so easy for me to answer the calling of my authentic self?

This is the question I asked myself, and what I discovered amazed me.

I am passionate about sharing my years of training…

Travels to Thailand and the study of Thai Massage.

Magical experiences in New Zealand, exploring the power of healing with hot white stones amplifying dreams and visions, and connecting with spirit guides and the feminine energies of the cosmic stars.

Diving into the energy of Chi Gong taught by a Master Teacher.

Reiki. Acupressure. Study of Tui Nu That supports the body's own healing process.

My time in Japan was spent studying Belly dancing, hatha yoga, levitating meditation and walking on hot coals. Mind over matter experiences

Experiencing laughter yoga with the creator and laughing for no reason increases breathing and lowers stress and has positive effects on wellbeing.

And so much more.

The fascination of being in my body and the ancient wisdom of people seeking to know the body and healing of the body became my passion.

Today, I see these experiences brought me to an awakening of my own feeling body. And learning ways truly own my authentic expression. And find my purpose in art.

> *It is time to set free and have the courage to live your creative life.*
> *Live each moment to the fullest and embrace your creativity.*
> *Being an artist and staying true to our authentic selves is*
> *a decision that comes from within.*
> *We are creative souls on a journey,*
> *and pursuing our dreams is essential.*
> *Take one step today toward your dream, no matter how small.*
> *It's time to bring all the pieces of your abandoned self*
> *together and follow your inspiration.*

As a child, I was innately guided to healing through the power of nature. My first memories are of my two-year-old self wandering across a country highway road… to the creek and deep into the full-bloomed mustard field… immersing myself in a sea of 3-foot-tall chartreuse stems and bright yellow blooms. Maybe it was the color that drew me in. Or maybe it was my innate knowledge of the medicinal qualities of the energy of this plant? Maybe it came from a prior lifetime? Or from the earth herself. I truly do not know.

But the heart of the healer was embraced. This became my purposeful path.'

Nature is infinitely creative.
It always produces the possibility of new beginnings.
—Marianne Williamson

Are you ready to transform your life?

Embarking on a journey of self-discovery can unlock your true potential, freeing your creativity and empowering you to live a life that reflects your core values and beliefs.

I found a passion that flourished in the exploration
of my version of what it would mean to be impassioned by the
transformational art of healing.

Vivid imagination became the palette of creating my world. It was not always easy; I was raised in the 70s as a latchkey kid by a single mom, living from day-to-day, sometimes on food stamps. No, life wasn't always easy. But there were things where I quickly found a respite away from the concerns. Art and creativity were my favorite pastimes, as were spending hours cutting out magazines and creating a vision board.

These experiences with art and creativity helped me overcome my challenges as a latchkey kid.

Being immersed in the feeling body, like putting on a record player, dancing with my sister, and giggling about the songs we would dance to. Or the richness of long, hot summer days, buttery cake batter, juicy watermelon, sweet/sour lemonade made from our own lemon bush, and add of a spoonful of sugar, and the neighbor's pool, Kool-aide, and pizza. Reflecting on my childhood shaped my views on creativity and resilience.

During the hot summer nights, we used to sleep outside under the blanket of stars and the moon. During the day, we would put on circus shows and performances with the kids in our neighborhood. We had plenty of time and freedom to do what we wanted until the streetlights turned on unless it was a nighttime hide-and-seek game. It was always wild and fun.

As the season shifted into autumn, we enjoyed the changing colors of the leaves that fell like a blaze of crimson, gold, and orange hues. We rake the leaves into intricate patterns, creating embellished labyrinths, spirals, and magical trails. Every step on the morning dew grass was a crunch underfoot, bringing the smell of earth and fresh falling leaves closer to something exciting and unknown.

We would recycle our old gifts, hide them in treasure hunts, and relish the joy of discovery and play. These moments of imagination and discovery were priceless. During these moments, we found significant expansion in our discovery of play. I remember being fearless while riding my horse to the river after a pouring winter rain and swimming with her. I had pure trust in my strength, body wisdom, and total respect for my horse, Sharon. She allowed me to hang on to her tail as she swam. These were the moments I cherished the most.

Creativity is a powerful tool that guides and
supports us through tough times.
By observing and witnessing ourselves,
we can start a journey of living an active, creative life.

Creativity is supported by embodiment practices such as awareness, movement, breath, and sound. These are avenues to body wisdom and inspiring creativity.

As an alchemist, you know that resetting your dreams with daily gratitude and reflection before bed is essential.

Imagine waking up feeling refreshed, energized, and focused.

Art flow supports your inner wisdom.
Listen to your heart. It will guide you and serve as your muse,
mentor, and mastermind. The transformation begins when we
embrace our creativity and start setting up space for it, one day
at a time. In the meantime, we can use a pen and notebook to
doodle, dream, and clear our minds.

You start your day by tuning your mind and body as an instrument to harmonize perfectly with your creative surroundings. Gratitude lets you connect with your inner wisdom, guiding you throughout the day. With a clear mind and a grounded heart, you are free to move forward with purpose and direction. By unlocking your potential with embodiment practices you are empowered to release emotional blockages and awaken your mind, body, and spirit and shed light on the shadow.

Affirmations can support our subconscious.
Nature can inspire our soul, and embodied movements
such as walking, yoga, and dancing can uplift our spirits."

These Practices Lead to Body Wisdom and Inspire Creativity.

There are many activities to choose from, like yoga, dance, mindfulness, and breathing exercises that help connect the mind and body.

- Meditation supports clearing the mind and calming the body.
- Taking walks in and around nature, practicing yoga movements or dance, and creating art or writing all help release stress, support cognition, and ground the body-mind.
- Nurture your creative nature. Practicing embodiment routines can help us feel clarity, more alive, and free.

These embodiment practices can lead to discovering more about oneself, healing, and personal growth. Our natural intuition has a lot of power and can guide us to heal. We all possess an innate ability to be creative and are inherently attracted to nature's immense power. By spending time in nature, we can tap into its healing power and find what we need to heal.

What inspires us to create?
What is the difference between inspiration and intuition?
What motivates you to create?

We are inspired by what we see, a certain someone, or a muse. We could find it by being around other artists or free writing. It begins by trusting your intuition and bravely allowing yourself to try new things.

Here are a few tools to help you to change up your routine and begin to see the world differently:

- Write with the other hand in your journal.
- Ask yourself what you are avoiding.
- Listen into the space often called the shadow, the space that's scared and is trying to protect you.

The way of Artistry of Alchemy is a path that allows us to explore our creativity and the inner world; this journey is about self-discovery, empowerment, and living a consciously brave, fulfilling, inspiring, and creative life.

The alchemist's journey, from frustration to inspiration, highlights the transformative power of adopting a mindset focused on creative liberation. The alchemist's practice recognizes the value of play, messy experimentation, and exploration in cultivating an environment that fosters creativity.

The urge to express and live a more inspired life,
shifted in 2020 into a state of opportunities,
forcing me to ask myself,
"If not now, when?"

I suddenly overcame my fear of making mistakes
and striving for perfection.
No more excuses.

As a young woman, I was drawn to becoming certified in body-centric practices. The world of yoga, dance, breathwork, meditation, and hands-on healing moved well beyond a hobby. It became the foundation of my trailblazing commitment to creatively expressing through the sacred arts and work in the field of somatic practices, and the body became a canvas.

My intuition was calling me into why I was here.

It is easy because it is who I am.

I am led by spirit.

My feeling body intelligence calms when I open to my authentic wisdom self.
The knowledge of innate wisdom moves me in this direction of being.

I see life in pictures.

I connect the dots.
Color expresses life through me, and like a lotus, I open.

My spirit shines.

Ease of life begins to flow.

The path is clear to create. I land in deepened trust.

It is easy for me to answer my calling.

It is the right thing to do:
Be authentic, creative, healing, and calming to the nervous system.

Let us awaken our passions and creativity.

To design your life…
to see your authentic power…
to embrace transformation…
This is becoming an artist of alchemy.
And I know this to be the path of unbridled creativity.

The way of the creative alchemist symbolizes insight, transformation, and intelligence. It is success expressed in love. It is honoring the power of quietude over the noise of a rambling, unsettled, agitated, distracted mind. And a realization of the creative essence that's only accessed through stillness over constant movement.

Understanding your power gives you way
to take action on your quest.
Be unapologetic.
Rise with it, and don't dim your light;
this is your life to shine.
You are unique. You are a miracle!
Find and explore what delights you and go for it.
Through the creative process, you will give yourself time and space.

What is whimsical and magical to you?
How can you surround yourself with this beauty?

Authentic, unbridled creativity symbolizes an inner environment that flourishes in confidence. Acceptance of all of it… awareness of all distractions… those things that steal your attention away from the callings of your heart… the source of your creativity.

Don't look outside yourself. Drop into the heart.
Let go of the how. Allow life to reveal its gifts.
It is the beauty of noticing.
It is the power of transforming doubt into love.
Happiness always comes from listening to your heart

and embracing the artistry of alchemy.

Love all your path of creation… Let yourself be supported and strong.

Allow the past to give you strength. Lean into the present moment.

The past cannot be changed.

But the past can become the creative wisdom to inform an empowered future.

> *"The creative act is not hanging on,*
> *but yielding to a new creative movement.*
> *Awe is what moves us forward."*
> —Joseph Campbell

Find the freedom of realizing all you have experienced and all you have come through as wisdom teachings designed to bring you to this moment and is guiding you to where you desire to go.

Are you willing to speak gently to your inner artist and give encouraging words? Or do you need a booming loudspeaker to remember your magnificence?

This is you, A bright source of creative flow!

Are you willing to love, look into your eyes, and say I love you… I know I am a spiritual, intelligent, radiant source of creative love!

When we realize our unique, authentic self as nature, we stay true, and the power of self-direction is revealed. Every moment is a new beginning; find wonderment in the beauty of nature.

- *Could nature be the answer for inspiration?*
- *Are you living in the infinite power of now?*
- *Are you aware that you are nature?*
- *How will knowing that you are a part of nature shift you to create?*

Keep on keeping on.
Say Yes to your dreams and visions; you got this.
Keep on keeping on with creativity and manifesting
your life because you say so.
I believe in my art and soul, so I am moving forward.

Commit to begin by:

- Access the power of your emotions so they fuel you rather than paralyze you.
- Allow your creative potential to speak to you through journaling.
- Explore what sparks joy.
- Deepen the awakening of your body through embodied practices that support your creative flow.
- Live in inspiration.
- Devote yourself to increasing self-esteem, self-love, and self-care.
- Revel in newfound courage and clarity, gain confidence through movement, and promote well-being.
- Rekindle your creative birthright.
- Be Brave!

In the words of Georgia O'keefe:

"To create one's world in any of the arts takes courage.
I decided to start anew, to strip away what I had been taught.
I decided that if I could paint that flower on a huge scale,
you could not ignore its beauty. The days you work are the best."

After reading her words, I realized that courage is simply the act of loving oneself.

So, I ask you:

- *Are you ready to stand up for your heart and passions and pursue a life as a creative?*

- *Are you willing to give it your all and live with wonder and amazement?*
- *What does that life look like for you?*
- *Will you act towards achieving it today?*

When we move toward our creativity, we move toward our Creator. We find ourselves becoming more creative when we seek to become more spiritual. Our creativity and spirituality are so closely interconnected that they are, in effect, the same thing.
—Deepak Chopra

Art making feels like time standing still, and I am neither past nor future; I am in the infinite now. When I feel the creator spirit move me and it all aligns, I feel so divinely connected to the power of innate wisdom, an intelligence of world mysteries.

What have you moved towards that was creatively divine?

Do you feel that your creativity is spiritual? If so, what is an example?

When did you feel closely interconnected through writing or painting?

Embracing my iconic power has changed how I see things.
It has impacted me in ways that I had only dreamt of.
Now, I know I am not dreaming. Because I am living the dream.

I now know that iconic power is to be the artist of my own life. This one mere simple acknowledgment opens my heart and soul's work. Once I experienced this kind of authentic flow, I knew true courage. This courage gives me the focus and energy to fulfill my dreams.

Art: It's our connection to the world…
our innate language that carries the power to
express our iconic human experience.

Becoming an Artistry of Alchemy teaches us ways to:

- Honor our own creative wisdom.
- Dissolve creative blocks.
- Lift the ceiling of one's thinking.
- Access authentic expression.
- Ignite natural motivation.
- Empower a commitment to live into the capacities of your inner creative artist.
- Make healthy and wise choices.
- Allow a natural curiosity to open a playful spirit.
- Embrace new potentials and allow them to be realized.

We can access our artistic alchemist power by asking questions that ignite the heart and soul of our creative destiny.

Creativity is inspired by daily practice. That's why the first dedicated step is to create a space that's your own. It's like a lifeline to committing to action, allowing yourself the time and space to be creative radiance. It's time to get prepared. Clear out the old and allow in the new.

I once read about a woman who lived in an eight-by-eleven room in New York City. Even in the smallest living spaces, she anchored in an experience to create with a small wooden table and a meditation pillow she picked up at a second-hand store. Another example is that of acclaimed mythologist Joseph Campbell, who I once read traveled with a 'special' ink pen and journal that marks his sacred creative space. The point is your space is your space... regardless of the size... or... *Imagine now where you can create a space.*

A space where you can use your imagination often.
Value your creativity.
Give yourself permission to dream.

It was Yayoi Kusama who said: *"A polka-dot has the form of the sun, which is a symbol of the energy of the whole world and our living life, and also the form of the moon, which is calm."*

For me, this artist stands for individuality. Her power is her uniqueness. A dot says it all. Imagine finding your passion in a dot. And this leads to tremendous passion in your life. It is time to connect the dots…

I encourage you to follow suit and be inspired. Doodle with dots. Are you ready to *'dot it out'*? Just do it! Imagine all the dots like a treasure map that will fuel your soul and passions. Create your own universe.

Allow yourself the intimacy, time, and space to acknowledge all you truly desire to create with a willingness to know what no longer supports. That's why the second dedicated step is a commitment to clear boundaries and making the space for your creative imagination to soar!

What are three things that distract you from creating?

"You Can't Use Up Creativity, the More You Use the More You Have."
—Maya Angelou

Making a commitment to your creativity opens the heart to your soul.

What if your creativity is your gift back to the universe?
Can you imagine all you could create if you kept going?
How could being more curious fuel your creativity?

Your creativity is your unique signature. What if your spark ignites a positive change in the world?

Declare: Yes. Yes Universe. Give yourself a sense of direction.

Consider, what is ONE ACTION you can take right now that will lead you to that which you most desire to create?

*Don't wait any longer. Allow yourself to experience the
breakthroughs you've longed for.
Remember, creativity is food for the soul.*

Authenticity is the doorway to higher creativity and an expansive, creative future. As you envision your life as an Artist of Alchemy, consider ways to actualize your own authentic expression. The key is consistency and dedication in establishing a practice to amplify a more productive and embodied creative life where art meets spirituality meets transformation. This is the way we can become more embodied, connected to the core of our natural creative beings, and find direction in our intuition. Map out your vision. Utilize play of the imagination.

We can move through obstacles on our path to self-growth and cultivate self-love: By remembering that everything is energy, even our thoughts... and by stimulating the senses, nature supports a profound connection and strengthens the creative soul. Here we find ways that refreshes, inspires, and offers vast beauty, serenity, and healing qualities.

*"Art is standing with one hand extended into the universe
and one hand extended into the world, and letting ourselves
be a conduit for passing energy."*
—Albert Einstein

Begin now: Commit to become an artist of alchemy. The path of an Artist of Alchemy is one paved in authentic creative power. Reclaim your creativity and relationship to time and space. Taking the time to slow down. Shifting and creating a container to set boundaries, get back in touch. Take time to look deep, discern the shadow self, and work with all aspects of self.

Most of all, remember:

This is about loving all of you. You are worthy of it all.

About CeCe Sanchez

CeCe is the creator of the Artistry of Alchemy, an expressive collection of transformational embodied practices. For over three decades she has supported individuals' emotional processes through art, mindfulness, journaling, and meditation. An impassioned teacher she nurtures community and intentional creativity through Artistry of Alchemy transformational journeys and retreats that include laughter, dance, circles, art creation, and movement.

The approach to healing through art and intentional creativity is empowering, and CeCe seeks to elevate, awaken, and support the authentic self by accessing higher creativity.

She believes that creativity is a birthright and our natural way of expressing ourselves, and it matters because it is how we give back our gifts to the world. Creativity inspires new ways of seeing and helps one to be more alive, motivated, and fulfilled. CeCe's work encourages play and self-discovery to recover one's natural, authentic self in tune with nature and provides a space to fall in love with oneself. It is CeCe's philosophy that when we are in love, we can heal and see others as ourselves and how we all belong.

The Artistry of Alchemy is inspirational and supports navigating the creative heart.

For more about CeCe Sanchez and her work visit:
www.CeCeSanchez.com

Dedication

This book is dedicated to my Mom, my Auntie, and my
daughters — all women with resilient spirits —
each has weathered difficult times
and found their way in our world and shine by example.

To the women who have become my true friends, heart
sisters who have stood beside me, sharing their wisdom, and
beautiful hearts as I have learned to let my own light shine.

Dedicated to women around the world who are feeling that
inner prompting and knowing there is something more.
May the spark of your soul radiantly shine as you step into your
worthiness, deep inner joy, recognizing your worth and value.

~Becky Norwood

Chapter 5

Let Your Soul Shine

It is better to walk in light than to dance in darkness.
The inner light shines from love, compassion, and faith.
If there is light in your heart, there can be no darkness in your soul.

Written by Becky Norwood

Often, our world today can feel tumultuous and disconcerting. And yet, in spite and despite all of the unrest, there is one thing we DO have the ability to control… and that is ourselves.

I am quite sure that not one of us has NOT gone through truly rough times. The times that are often considered the dark night of the soul. Yet through these dark, soul-wrenching experiences, a spark inside us becomes a glowing ember and an inner flame. A flame unwilling to be snuffed out.

Growing up, I was at the mercy of a highly abusive father. He was a Jekel and Hyde – multiple personality type person who could and did charm the socks off of anyone he came in contact with. As a child, we first were Lutheran, then he insisted we become Rosicrucian, then Jehovah's Witness, then Catholic, then Mormon. And every time, he would advance quickly up to positions of responsibility… until people disappointed him (or quite possibly they caught on to his abusive tendencies). Either way, we would be instructed to ride along — forsake all friendships and move on to the next BEST thing.

There were many instances where a tragedy in the U.S. (suspicious things like train derailments and the Oklahoma bombings). would prompt an investigative visit from the FBI, due to his radical hate-filled reproach of U.S. politics.

Combine that with the constant reminder of being ugly, stupid, and worth NOTHING, which was the mantra that he ranted constantly, not just to me but to my siblings and even my mother – and you get a family that was in a state of confusion at all times. Mental, physical, emotional, and sexual abuse was the norm. The little girl in me lost the magic of make-believe and joy around four years old, and it took me well into adulthood to awaken the recognition of the goodness within me.

As the oldest daughter, I was responsible for my siblings. I was put in charge of making sure they were doing what they were supposed to do. Fail at that – even at eight years old, and it meant not only watching them get beat senseless, but it also meant the same for me, and often worse. His children were his slaves, in many more ways than one. Play was seldom allowed. We were alienated from all extended family. He moved us far away from them and allowed no contact. Entering the teen years, as he sensed the slightest sense of rebellion, there was the incessant threat that he knew how to end our life.

It was not that there was not a spark left inside me.
It was that I did not know how to access it.
I felt enslaved and in deep, raw fear for my life.

As happens to likely most all women who grow up in such an environment, we do not have a healthy barometer of what is healthy and normal… we grew up in an abnormally unhealthy environment. So as we enter adulthood we see life through a dysfunctional lens and go on to attract the same into our life.

My first marriage was no exception. I married a man much like my father, but my awareness… that deep inner yearning and knowingness that there has to be something better… was creating a restlessness within my soul. I was no longer willing to listen to the *'shit talk'*, the undermining of worthiness, the constant beratement, and the threats.

That marriage lasted less than three years — providing me with two beautiful daughters. I was six months pregnant with my second baby and the oldest was thirteen months old when I entered single-parenthood and went on to raise them completely on my own — without support. He chose not to be a part of their lives.

In the meantime, my father chose to take his life, unable to deal with the guilt of his horrible behavior.

I chose not to get involved in another relationship until my daughters were grown. I was too afraid I would attract the same into my life.

The road was tough for a while, but in those years of raising my daughters alone, afforded a freedom to explore what happiness looked like. I explored many religions; I explored many forms of what was then considered New Age. I read voraciously, spent time in nature, and spent lots of time with my children, intent on raising wholesome, well-rounded women. All brought me awareness, and the promptings of my soul. And then, I took an amazing class on the power of the mind – and viola – it opened… and EXPLODED many doors of awareness.

The light in my heart, the spark in my soul grew brighter. I was unwilling to let the ugly of the past take root and destroy my future.

I remember learning to laugh! Sound strange? I had become so serious that when people around me told jokes, I could not laugh. I didn't see anything funny. Now, it is a different story – I get to enjoy some amazing belly laughs – and what a healer laughter is.

As I maneuvered through life, raising my daughters, I made my fair share of mistakes, but those mistakes were teaching me and preparing me for what life could be and was supposed to be!

All that said, I know beyond all doubt that I do not hold a corner on the market when it comes to the pain I experienced. Many others have experienced the same or worse.

> *"Owning our story can be hard but not as difficult as spending our lives running from it. Exploring and embracing our vulnerabilities is risky but not nearly as dangerous as giving up on love, belonging, and joy—the experiences that make us the most vulnerable. Only when we are brave enough to explore the darkness will we discover the infinite power of our light."*
> **— Brene Brown**

I've observed that often, the women who had the troubled, tough childhoods, are the ones, who today are leading the world in unique and heartfelt ways. They stumbled their way through finding themselves as they stepped into adulthood and, in time, they discovered their strengths and special gifts.

I believe that the inherent goodness of humanity is awakening and that it is time to shine our light out to the world. From the depths of our souls, we can choose to shine. The world needs us. WE need us! We need ourselves to embrace the life that makes our heart sing.

Think about it. Which feels better? Succumbing to the heartache and sadness that once colored our world or choosing to live a joyous and rewarding life?

> *Living our SOUL SHINE opens our inner world*
> *to possibilities and magic.*

We have an inner glow... a SOUL SHINE... that does not go unnoticed by others. When our personalities become aligned with our souls, our power to attract the desires of our hearts is magnified and optimized. As we begin to live our lives on purpose and joyfully, we create a ripple effect that makes a difference in our lives and the lives of others simply by being ourselves.

It does not require us to be a Mother Teresa *or to be what society has told us we should be* – though if that is what your soul is speaking to you… listen to it.

So what is SOUL SHINE?

SOUL SHINE begins with a glimmer of recognition. A deep inner knowing that there is something more to life. There is something more to YOU.

SOUL SHINE is that inner stirring that wants to be expressed in life. At first, it can feel a bit disconcerting, like a restlessness that won't go away. A gentle knowingness that begins with a little spark that fans into a glowing ember and then a flame when acknowledged.

How Can We Awaken Our SOUL SHINE?

It begins with recognizing yourself. It starts with stopping long enough within our days to listen and watch for clues. It starts with stepping into worthiness. It begins with the willingness to recognize who YOU are and what you stand for.

And often, it is grace through surrender, self-compassion, and self-love. Love – for ourselves can become the master healer of our lives.

No matter what life has brought us, the good, the bad, the ugly, we simply cannot change what has transpired already. What is done is done. Looking back, other than to reflect on how far you have come, and what you learned from those times, will not change anything.

The change happens when we realize that all we have is the here and now. Is it time to feel our way into our SOUL SHINE?

It is time to make a *Sacred Agreement* with ourselves to let your SOUL SHINE.

It is through the power of our *Sacred Agreements* that our lives become infused with focus, meaning and direction.

Life has shown me that swimming in the memories and letting the clouds overpower me – is far more painful than letting my SOUL SHINE.

Think about it. We have all heard that it takes more muscles to frown than to smile. With good reason! It certainly feels far better to be happy than sad, to shine than to live a life of dullness and grief.

Sadness and despair become an engrained, deeply entrenched pattern or habit.

And if that is the same for you to a greater or lesser degree, let us explore the world of possibility together.

Don't look away from those moments. Lean into the messiness, the craziest of challenges, the times of feeling lost or deep in self-doubt. Why? Because those moments illuminate your RADIANT LEGACY... your radiant potentials... your untapped skills, undiscovered possibilities, and under-estimated passions. They lead you to discover what makes **YOUR** SOUL SHINE all that it is.

Dig in. Consider. Embrace. Then, let's link arms and radiate a NEW feminine creative consciousness into the world. Because, SOUL SHINING, incredible (amazing) woman, is what the world needs most now.

Are you open to the idea of letting your SOUL SHINE? Are you willing to grow beyond what perhaps has defined your life till now?

If so, these steps will begin to open the doors and windows of your life.

It begins with asking yourself some pointed questions. But be aware that asking the questions also requires you to listen within for the answers. To hear those answers, we often need to get quiet and pay attention to the sparks of recognition and knowingness that well from within.

Ask yourself:

- *Where do I want to go in life?*
- *What do I desire to create for myself?*
- *Why do I desire this?*
- *How dedicated am I to let my life be incredibly remarkable and spectacular?*
- *How great am I willing to let my life become?*

It is time to shine the light on the shadows of our soul and get real and raw with ourselves. It's time to excavate the roots behind why we are not living the life we are meant to live. The origins of this often dwell in feelings of unworthiness, deservingness, stuckness, and even fear. Fear of change. Fear of letting go.

Ask yourself:

- *Am I underestimating what I am truly willing to receive?*
- *Am I deserving of more?*
- *Am I dreaming big, rich, and juicy enough to flame the spark within me?*
- *Is it time to replace all the un's of negativity with a new energy?*

So now, let's talk about how to implement SOUL SHINE Practices to discover, uncover, and reveal the true you — waiting to ignite that flame into an ember and then into a fire that lights your world.

"When you step into who you really are, everything works."

SUPERPOWER PRACTICES
TO
IGNITE YOUR SOUL SHINE

What are your superpowers? Do you tap into them daily? What would be a useful superpower in your everyday life?

If you could choose a superpower, what would it be?

The following suggestions are not to overwhelm you. Explore and find what works for YOU. The are meant to spark your SOUL SHINE and expand your mind past the identity that mis-created your childhood and beyond.

It is meant to help you reframe old beliefs, dissolving an outdated mindset that diminishes your creative powers.

Here are just a few Superpower Practices:

1. The Power of the Pause

The power of the pause is well researched. It promotes relaxation and refreshes you for hours. Both the outer noise and the often more incessant inner noise can keep us from finding the answers we seek.

Power Pause Practice:

1. Place your feet on the floor and your hand on your thighs and close your eyes. And if you're driving, just keep your eyes steady
2. For a moment, bring your attention way down to your feet. Just notice your feet on the ground, notice your seat in the chair, notice your hands on your legs.

3. Now find your heart beating, find your pulse somewhere in your body. Bring your mind, your attention, into your body as quickly as possible.

4. Now place a light attention on the natural rhythm of your breath. With your mind resting on your breath, you may start to notice a sense of ease. You may start to notice, as you exhale fully, that there's a little bit less tension. A little bit less noise.

5. There's not much to do when all you need to do for the next few moments is notice your feet, notice your hands, notice your heartbeat and notice your breath, landing on any one of those areas in your body is just perfect. A perfect way to take a pause.

6. And now open your eyes if they have been closed and just notice what a few moments of pause can do. Our bodies are magnificent, brilliant, stabilizing systems when we give our body and our mind the opportunity to balance and align.

2. Surrender

Surrender is what worthiness looks like when potential is realized. I invite you to step into the wholeness of worthiness.

Every one of us at some point encounters a situation that rocks the foundation of who we are and what we think we can bear—something that pushes us past our limits. Sometimes it's a situation we've lived with for a long time and sometimes it's a sudden event that overwhelms us and for which our usual coping strategies are useless. Our mind tries to control everything it comes in contact with. And then comes a time, a situation, when we can't keep fighting, either because it's too painful, or because we finally know at a body/heart level that it's futile and some other as of yet unknown path is needed.

Surrender begins here, where all other strategies end. It's waking up to realize that all the strategies have failed and we're plum out of new ones.

Surrender Practice: To practice, we simply surrender into what is, right now. We drop into our direct experience, what we are sensing, feeling, living in this moment. We agree to feel life, as it is, now, without our mind adding, taking away, manipulating, or doing anything whatsoever to it.

Ask/Invite Yourself:

- *What is it like right now if I let everything be just as it is?*
- *If I don't do anything to it, what is my actual experience in this moment?*
- Feel this, here, now.

Surrender, at its core, is the willingness to meet life as it is, to stop fighting with or trying to change what is so, right now. And remarkably, no matter what the catalyst, or whether it is a moment's surrender or a lifetime's, the result or gift that accompanies it remains the same: relief, <u>gratitude</u>, grace, and sometimes even joy.

3. Trust

Trust is a superpower that is often under-valued. At the foundation of self-confidence and the basis of boldness and self-assertion is a deep inner trust. If trust shuts you down – and it keeps you under lock and key, it is time to unlearn old beliefs. *Why?* Because your current ideas of trust (as in you can only trust yourself) holds you back from experiencing your real, authentic self.

Trust births from a core acknowledged truth: *You are a divine being in physical form.* When you're focused on that major detail, every limitation previously attributed to trusting yourself and others spontaneously melts away.

4. Gratitude

Gratitude is a positive emotion that involves being thankful and appreciative and is associated with several mental and physical health benefits. When you experience gratitude, you feel grateful for something or someone in your life and respond with feelings of kindness, warmth, and other forms of generosity.

So what does gratitude look like? How do you know if you are experiencing a sense of gratitude? Expressing your appreciation and thanks for what you have can happen in a number of different ways. For example, it might entail:

- Spending a few moments thinking about the things in your life that you are grateful for
- Stopping to observe and acknowledge the beauty of wonder of something you encounter in your daily life
- Being thankful for your health
- Thanking someone for the positive influence they have in your life
- Doing something kind for another person to show that you are grateful
- Paying attention to the small things in your life that bring you joy and peace
- Meditation or prayer focused on giving thanks

5. Passion

What is your passion? Passion is a powerful motivator and the essence of commitment. Passion is what stirs us, the fuel for will, the Soul Shine, the fire within. Passion is the seed from which commitment blossoms. Is it time to dream bigger and dance with the possibilities?

"There is not passion to be found playing small, in settling for a life that is less that the one you are capable of living."
—Nelson Mandela

Following your passion will allow even more creative potential to pave the way to heal, to teach, to inspire and love.

6. Forgiveness

"It's one of the greatest gifts you can give yourself. Forgive.
Forgive everybody."
— Maya Angelou

This important lesson from Maya Angelou is about the importance and power that the act of forgiveness can bring to someone. More importantly – what it can do to help your Soul Shine!

Choosing to forgive someone is an extraordinarily powerful gift, to yourself… first and foremost. In my case, forgiveness of my father did not come till long after he had passed on. But forgiving him is something I did for myself. It alleviated the constant festering of ugly memories and years of toxic anger, guilt, shame and fear that had built up inside me. I forgave him for my own wellbeing.

It does NOT mean that I condone what he did to myself and my family. It means that there is something inherently strong in being able to say, 'I forgive you', and truly mean it, yields positive benefits to every facet of your live. Forgiveness is good, so go spread it in your own life as much as you can.

There are so many other superpowers that come into play that will spark that Soul Shine within. It is my heartfelt hope and passion that you will begin to explore what makes your Soul Shine!

Many blessings…

About Becky Norwood

Becky Norwood is a multi-published #1 International Bestselling author, speaker, & book publishing expert.

Her passion is helping women discover, uncover and recover their Soul Shine, find their authentic voice, and lead in the world with radiant passion.

She is widely recognized for the empowering and intuitive way she guides others to weave storytelling into a powerful way to build a legacy and gateway for the healing and growth of themselves, their families and for the world. In sharing authentic, vulnerable, stories they are able to impact others to ignite that flame into an ember and then into a fire that lights their own world. She is an advocate for the positive that comes from letting your SOUL SHINE.

Facebook: https://www.facebook.com/SpotlightBookPublishing
LinkedIn: https://www.linkedin.com/in/beckybnorwood/
Instagram: https://www.instagram.com/spotilghtpublishinghouse/
Website: https://spotlightpublishinghouse.com
Email: becky@spotlightpublishinghouse.com

Dedication

This chapter is dedicated to my beloved mother,
whose love, humor, and strength
has been my truest example of an
Iconic and Amazing Woman.

~Rocio Ortiz Luevano

Chapter 6

The Awakening of Divine Grace

"Pray to Mother Mary. She is your Spirit Guide.
She will help you through all times.
Also meditate and open yourself to
Eastern philosophies, Buddhism, yoga.
Read Thich Nhat Han and Marianne Williamson.
Reconnect with your femininity."

Written by Rocio Ortiz Luevano

These words were spoken to me almost 15 years ago but remain vividly palpable in my heart and memory. It was my very first encounter with an Intuitive Healer. That session left me with a sense of peace, purpose, and bold empowerment. I had never felt anything like it. It prepared me to make profound and long-lasting changes in my life and ready to heal a long list of subtle and unspoken traumas including generational trauma, early childhood trauma, trauma experienced through the passing of my beloved husband, and trauma experienced simply by being a woman in the world. The path ahead at the time was not entirely clear, but faith in myself and the future fortified by my spiritual practice was all I needed to forge ahead.

Reaching this pivotal stage in my life did not happen overnight. It took the unceasing and loving support of friends, family, and years of therapy to lay the groundwork for the change.

The process of therapy pushed me to explore the vastness of my feelings and to fully connect with them.

Therapy created the space and time to pause and go inward, to reflect on the subconscious as well as an opportunity to make changes and shifts in my life-giving words to my experiences allowing myself to be vulnerable with my feelings. To appreciate the value of all my emotions and to really listen to what was being uncovered by them. Therapy was the safe space where I was encouraged to examine the optimal and less than optimal choices I had made over the years, and to find forgiveness for myself and others. It allowed me to find compassion, kindness and understanding for myself. But most importantly, I learned to make myself a priority.

My evolution and healing through therapy would not only help me; but I could foresee that through my own healing process I would also be equipped to guide my son, who was and continues to be my greatest source of motivation. It would equip me to prepare him for life and for his future. A future that would undoubtedly expose him to trauma and challenging circumstances. He would be guided to build his own resiliency and emotional strength for whatever should come.

After my encounter with intuitive healing and therapy, my life started to change very rapidly and take a new shape. Initially traveling through the dark night of the soul. For me, the dark night of the soul was rooted in a very difficult, nearly indescribable experience in my first marriage that created a deep wound and profound trauma... his incarceration, caring for our son, managing the home while maintaining focus for my work, looking after his dying father and heartbroken mother, and eventually, our separation and divorce. Going through a myriad of emotions and feelings. Navigating depression, rage, grief, guilt... I had many sleepless nights doubtful if I would be able to lift myself out of the darkness. I wondered. But I stayed with it.

It was as though I could hear Mother Mary say,
"Am I not here, I Who Am your Mother?"

One Saturday afternoon after a visit to the prison I listened to the whisper of my intuition which led me to the Cathedral of Our Lady of the Angels in Downtown LA. I made my way to the statue of Our Lady of Guadalupe, and I dropped to my knees. I pleaded "Mother, you don't have to fix my situation, just guide me, guide my way." The answers to my problems went beyond anything anyone could do, I needed to surrender them to the divine. After spending a long time in quiet reflection, I walked away with a knowing that all would be well and felt profound peace in my heart. When I arrived home a dear and thoughtful aunt was kind enough to gift me a CD of the rosary. Before that I had never really prayed the rosary, but I was grateful for her gift.

For the first time in my life, I really connected with Mother Mary, praying the rosary every morning and every night, asking her to guide me and light my path. Gradually the knots became untied, things just started to work themselves out, the darkness started to lift. I felt more hopeful. The Blessed Mother would remain ever protective and loving of me.

My desire and motivation for change was strong. A new me wanted to be birthed through this transformation. There was a shedding of the old as the new came forth. It was a spiritual depression which was giving way for a new life. A time of deep spiritual work, introspection, and healing.

Eventually my energy started to shift. I started to feel better. I focused on self-care and self-love. I was kind to my body. I exercised and started shedding the weight and the emotional baggage. I was in strong pursuit of spiritual growth, wisdom, and healing. I discovered Kundalini Yoga, a merging of spiritual and physical yoga. I was introduced to the healing shabad/prayer of So Purkh. I became a Reiki Healer and began practicing with my son. He enjoyed the practice and would ask me for Reiki as a bedtime routine. As he lay in bed, I would hover my hands over his chakras to bring balance and healing to his energy centers. I would invoke Mother Mary and pray the Hail Mary as I provided Reiki. He would quickly settle in and relax. Her presence and loving energy were palpable as she guided healing.

Praying So Purkh created major shifts in my life. Shifts and changes began integrating so quickly, that my life took on new shapes and forms. I experienced healing of relationships, meeting like-minded people, financial stability, feeling hopeful and positive about the future. It was exciting and compelling for me, and it gave me more energy to stay with my spiritual practice. I was in awe of how quickly change took shape and it gave me the momentum to stay true to my spiritual practice.

So Purkh brought me to remember the words the intuitive healer shared with me when she suggested that I explore my feminine nature. What I discovered was the sacred feminine within. A feminine spirit with a great capacity for love, forgiveness, openness, communion and so much more. A sacred feminine that shows great power through love and kindness. The embodiment of Mother Mary herself. Nothing that I could ever have imagined and yet so rich with possibilities. I was surprised to discover that there was so much of my feminine nature that had been denied, forgotten, and overlooked. Through this practice I began to feel my intuition more deeply. My intuition began to open even more. My self-care and my nurturing were changing my life. My ability to listen to the words others shared became more attuned and reflective.

Whenever I chanted So Purkh I really felt the difference. The energy became much lighter, the heaviness lifted. I was filled with compassion, forgiveness, and love.

Any conflicts or discord with men would resolve after I chanted So Purkh. My relationships with men changed as they became more peaceful and respectful. The men would become more compassionate and kinder… and if they weren't, they would drift away. It was during this time that I met my beloved husband, Alex. It was as though the universe/Source/Mother Mary said we have heard you and now we present you with the high-quality man you have been seeking for so long. My husband brought so much love and healing into my life. For the first time in my life, I felt seen, heard, valued, trusted, and understood by a man. He loved me for all that I was... the good, the bad, and in between... for my strengths and weaknesses and I loved him in the same ways. It was a beautifully nurturing time of my life.

After we married a Healer said to me, *"Your wedding ring has been blessed by Mother Mary herself."* I believed this to be true as I remembered the day of our wedding kneeling before the statue of Our Lady of Guadalupe thanking her and asking her to bless our marriage.

It was a beautiful period of my life when I found more inspiration and meaning in my professional life as well. At that point in my career, I was supervising a mental health program dedicated to supporting at risk mothers and very young children. A program which I loved and cherished. The focus was to support, empower and uplift women who had experienced trauma. I felt a deep level of compassion for these women who had intimate partner violence and those who had mental illness really pulled at my heartstrings. I also empathized with those who struggled with substance abuse. Our goal was to not only help these women become emotionally connected to their children but also to help support and create resilience for the children as well. In short, healing the mother to heal the child.

At some point I reflected and asked myself why I felt so compelled to help little children. The memories came rushing in and taking me back to remembering myself in kindergarten. It was the mid 1970's and as a child of Spanish speaking Mexican immigrant parents I felt nervous and intimidated by school. I remember attending an orientation meeting of some sort with my mother and asking her, "What are the teachers saying mom?", to which she replied, "I don't know." In my 5-year-old child's mind, I thought, *"How can she not know."* I was terrified realizing I would have to navigate an unknown environment on my own away from my mother without speaking the language.

I didn't know what it was called at the time, but all I knew was that I wanted to go home to my mother. To be held and comforted by her. Eventually I learned I was dealing with severe separation anxiety. But why the label? Instead of recognizing that I was a child who needed to be held, validated, and supported. So, when my emotions were too big for me, my instinct was to run out of the classroom, every chance I had, hoping to catch my mom before she left the school grounds. I didn't feel safe or understood and I also felt embarrassed knowing my peers would witness me in a state of dysregulation. I was terrified, scared, worried, anxious, sad. I felt hopeless and abandoned.

My parents were supportive, but I don't remember receiving any formal emotional support from the school. Something inside me told me this was not ok. I felt forgotten and isolated, like I didn't matter. Feeling like an eternity, I eventually acclimated and adapted to school. I was fortunate to have support and protective factors at home, most importantly love and guidance. These would help sustain me through those pivotal years.

I now know and understand that it takes courage to go to school and learn a new language...

I was worried I wouldn't be heard... that I wouldn't be able to understand and that I would not be understood. The root of what I do now is help parents understand their children and for their children to understand themselves... for parents to understand themselves.

I may not have known or been aware at the time, but I know and trust that Mother Mary was watching over me and protecting me during this time.

Along my journey of healing, pieces of my life started to come together. I was absolutely thrilled when my employer generously paid my way through the highly desired Napa Infant Parent Mental Health Fellowship, a prestigious 15 month post graduate program for people interested in expanding their knowledge of infant parent mental health. I knew it wouldn't be easy to juggle my full-time job, be mom, wife and participate in this academically rigorous program. But I was all in.

It was something I had been dreaming of doing for years. It threw me into an expanded field that felt uncomfortable and intimidating at times, but I also felt great enthusiasm and eagerness to learn. It was a beautiful and robust program which covered mental health, neurobiology and so much more. I learned about the impact of trauma on mothers and the developing brains of very young children. I became familiar with the work of Stephen Porges and his cutting-edge Polyvagal Theory which helps us understand the fight, flight and freeze response in our nervous system and how knowing this can inform the way we heal trauma. Looking back, I now see that I was learning to feel more love and compassion for the 5-year-old me, the scared child who would run out of the classroom looking for her mom.

I learned about Dr. Bruce Perry and his work with traumatized children and the importance of reaching and healing children as early and as young as possible. Most importantly I was struck by the idea that healing for all of us occurs when the body engages in rhythmic, patterned, repetitive, somatosensory experiences. Learning and taking all this information in brought everything into focus. The Kundalini yoga, dancing, movement, chanting So Purkh, praying the rosary, was doing so much more, it was helping me through my own healing at a physical, emotional, cellular, and spiritual level.

> *The convergence of my personal experience,*
> *my healing and my studies brought everything full circle.*
> *I came to understand that the struggles of the past*
> *were all a part of my evolutionary process.*
> *They were not missteps but stepping-stones*
> *leading me in a new direction of growth and self-discovery.*

The trauma I once experienced… the shock, the turbulence, and the grief… as well as the moments of doubt, frustration and disappointment were guiding me towards a full transformation of self.

The image that so often comes to mind is Our Lady of Guadalupe, Tonantzin, Mother Mary as she is known throughout the world.

*She embodies and represents the sacred feminine and her great
capacity for love, forgiveness, openness, and compassion.
She reminds us that we are all ICONIC and as such we all have
the capacity to transform as well as heal all past, present,
and future wounds and traumas of one's heart.
She has become the source, the reason and inspiration for my
iconic power. I also know and trust that she has been with me
throughout my entire life supporting me every step of the way.
Guiding and lifting me through the joy and through the pain.
She will remain ever present.*

My healing journey has been purposeful but not without struggle. Despite feeling profoundly guided, loved, and supported by Spirit, especially Mother Mary, there were moments where I felt deeply fearful of being sacrilegious of my Catholic faith. But in the end, I would feel guided to fully embrace all aspects of my spiritual growth while remaining the fullest and most authentic expression of myself. I remember once having a mystical experience while in a Kundalini yoga class. I noticed that the teacher was transforming. His face, his clothing changing color, turning into Guru Ram Das, in the Sikh tradition he was the fourth Sikh Guru and an important figure in Kundalini Yoga. Gradually the teacher transformed again, turning into Jesus. I couldn't believe my eyes, I was not psychotic or under the influence of anything... all I know is that this was confirmation... beyond religion, beyond tradition... we are all one.

In 2018 my spirituality was tested. My daughter/step-daughter Alexandria passed away unexpectedly at age 24. I was devastated and angry... she was such a loving and beautiful soul... I asked God how she could be taken so soon. Our entire family was shaken to the core over her loss. When I first started dating her father, Allie, as we affectionately called her, embraced me and accepted me into the family wholeheartedly. Not an easy thing for a young or adult child to do. As I mourned her loss, I came to appreciate all the beautiful gifts she left us. The memory of a beautiful, loving, and generous life.

A life, though brief, was a life well lived. My spirituality would give me the strength to carry on despite this painful loss.

Nothing could have prepared me for this…
the passing of my beloved.

On January 24, 2022, my beloved Husband Alex Luevano passed away. He became ill and I feel he remained heartbroken from losing our beautiful Allie. But losing him crushed my soul to pieces. Initially I felt like I was out of my body, disconnected, I felt rage, frustration, confusion, why us, why me? Another devastating loss. The pain was excruciating… feelings of abandonment, sadness, depletion, and numbness surfaced. There were moments where I even contemplated joining him. But instead, I wrote about and reflected on our time together… it gave me solace.

Before I met my husband, I wrote a list of attributes I was seeking in a companion. I knew the universe was listening, so I was very specific in my request. Whoever was to show up in my life needed to be the following:

Confident. Self-assured. Gracious. Compassionate. Kind.
Sensitive to the human spirit. Funny. Forgiving.
Humble and someone who loved his mother and family.
Someone who loved children.
Someone who enjoyed the outdoors and traveling.
Someone who made me laugh and allowed me to be me.

The man who showed up was the love and soul of my life. Although

our time together was brief, he made me incredibly happy. I was heartbroken by his loss yet eternally grateful to have loved such an incredible man.

During these times so many people came forth to support my son and me.

I felt unconditionally loved and supported, an unknown force gently, softly moving me along. Despite the pain, I knew I could access my spiritual tools, as well as seeking answers from my spiritual teachers and healers. I was reminded that I was not alone, and that my husband would always be watching over me. It was in these moments that I felt Mother Mary's presence.

Today I have come to realize that our life experiences, even those of great trauma, pain and grief can carry the greatest gifts of transformation, expansion, and wisdom.

I feel when we pause, bless, and have gratitude for all of our experiences, it liberates and propels us forward towards a deep healing. Allowing us to return to the simplicity of wholeness. Now more than ever I feel compelled and inspired to help other women find their own healing, find their own feminine gifts… to emerge and awaken through Divine Grace… to reveal their true, powerful and authentic selves.

I invite you to explore the words of the
So Purkh Prayer Mantra

Vaheguru Raag Aasaa Mehela Chauta So Purkh
From the Fourth Master Guru Ram Das

So purkh niranjan har purkh niranjan har agamaa agam apaaraa
Sabh dhiaaveh sabh dhiaaveh tudh jee har sachay sirajanhaaraa
Sabh jee-a tumaaray jee too(n) jee-aa kaa dataaraa
Har dhiaavaho santaho jee sabh dookh visaaranhaaraa
Har aapay thaakur har aapay sayvak jee
kiaa naanak jant vichaaraa //1//
Too(n) ghat ghat antar sarab nirantar jee har ayko purakh samaanaa
Ik daatay ik bhaykhaaree jee sabh tayray choj vidaanaa
Too(n) aapay daataa aapay bhugataa jee hao tudh bin avar na jaanaa
Too(n) paarbraham bayant bayant jee
tayray kiaa gun aakh vakhaanaa

Jo sayveh jo sayveh tudh jee jan naanak tin kurbaanaa //2//
Har dhiaaveh har dhiaaveh tudh jee say jan jug meh sukhvaasee
Say mukat say mukat bha-ay jin har dhiaa-
i-aa jee tin tootee jam kee phaasee
Jin nirbhao jin har nirbhao dhiaa-i-aa jee tin kaa bhao sabh gavaasee
Jin sayvi-aa jin sayvi-aa mayraa har jee tay har har roop samaasee
Say dhan say dhan jin har dhiaa-i-aa jee
jan naanak tin bal jaasee //3//
Tayree bhagat tayree bhagat bhandaar jee bharay biant bayantaa
Tayray bhagat tayray bhagat salaahan tudh
jee har anik anayk anantaa
Tayree anik tayree anik kareh har poojaa
jee tap taapeh japeh bayantaa
Tayray anayk tayray anayk parheh baho simrit
saasat jee kar kiri-aa khat karam karantaa
Say bhagat say bhagat bhalay jan naanak jee jo
bhaaveh mayray har bhagvantaa //4//
Too(n) aad purakh aparampar kartaa jee tudh jayvad avar na ko-ee
Too(n) jug jug ayko sadaa sadaa too(n) ayko
jee too(n) nihachal kartaa so-ee
Tudh aapay bhaavai so-ee varatai jee too(n) aapay kareh su ho-ee
Tudh aapay srisht sabh upaa-ee jee tudh aapay siraj sabh go-ee
Jan naanak gun gaavai karatay kay jee jo sabhasai kaa jaano-ee //5//

So Purkh that Primal God
I AM one with God
This is my true guru's gift
The primal one is perfectly pure
The primal God is perfect.
He is within all and beyond all
Everyone meditates.
All souls meditate on you Oh true creator
All souls are one with you.
All souls come from you.
O saints Meditate on God and all pains will fly away

God himself is the master
God himself is the servant
O Nanak everyone is empty-handed before him
You are in each beat of my heart and in all hearts
O Lord you are the One in Everyone
Some are givers and some are takers this is all your play
You are the giver and you are the receiver it is all you.
You are the God of all; endless and infinite
I have no words to describe your virtues
O Lord Nanak is a Sacrifice unto those
who serve and serve you forever.
Meditate on God meditate on God
and your soul will be at peace in this world.
Meditate on God and live free.
Live free and know the noose of death is meaningless.
Meditate on the fearless one,
The fearless God,
And Live free from fear.
Those who serve, O those who serve my Lord
Are one with Har (God) and they look divine.
Blessed O Blessed are they who meditate on Har (God)
Servant Nanak is a sacrifice to them
Devotion to you O devotion to you
is a treasure trove that ever overflows.
Your lovers, O your lovers praise you, my beloved, Forever and Ever.
For you, Just for you O Lord so many poojas are performed
and so many endlessly chant and discipline themselves.
For you, just for you O Lord so many read the smritis
and shastras they do kriyas and ceremonies.
Those lovers those lovers are sublime O Servant Nanak
Who please my beloved Lord God.
You are the primal One, the most awesome creator
of everything, there are none as great as you.
Throughout time and beyond time,
You are the One. The constant and true creator.

You do everything and everything happens according
to your will, you create the whole Universe.
You destroy it and You create it again.
Servant Nanak sings the praises of his beloved Lord
forever and ever and ever.
He is the Knower within all souls...

About Rocio Ortiz Luevano, LCSW

Rocio Ortiz Luevano is a Licensed Clinical Social Worker, Infant-Family and Early Childhood Mental Health Specialist, Reiki Practitioner, first generation Mexican-American and best-selling author.

Through neuroscience, spirituality and her personal story, Rocio encourages women to find their own strength and potential for inner healing. It is also through their own healing that they can powerfully create healing for their children and future generations.

For over twenty years, Rocio has served and supported vulnerable mothers and very young children in the Los Angeles area who have experienced and been affected by trauma or adversity. Her aim has been to foster emotional healing and empowerment, as well as ending generational trauma for mothers and babies. Her hope is to help them unearth their innate capacity for emotional healing as well as to help them discover healing through a personal spiritual practice.

Rocio stands for non-violent parenting, protection of children from trauma and the uncompromised respect for women. Her multitude of skills as a Clinician and Teacher including spiritually mindedness, Neuroscience informed, Trauma-informed and Reiki Healer, allows her to help people from a psycho-educational, neuroscientific and spiritual perspective.

Her vision is to help women who have experienced trauma or challenging situations to emerge, transform and embrace their freedom and simultaneously heal, protect and create resilience for their children.

For more information about Rocio Ortiz Luevano visit:

www.chiopsw@gmail.com
chiopsw on Instagram

Dedication

I dedicate this chapter to my Soul Sister Marie Soulière,
the embodiment of kindness and the courage it takes to fully
embrace oneself. She has been my unwavering pillar,
my greatest encourager and cheerleader, believing
in me long before I could believe in myself.
Marie truly sees me; Like a proud parent witnessing their child's
first achievement, Marie's pride in me surpassed my own.

Her nurturing kindness is a quality I learned to give myself
through her guidance, often reflecting on what Marie
would say or do during moments of self-judgment and
fear. She played a pivotal role in helping me blossom into
the beautiful authentic and unique soul that I am.

With Marie I've experienced the genuine essence of family.
Our connection transcends time and space, uniting us as
soul family. Our closeness isn't measured by distance ·
we are only a breath of consciousness apart.
Marie is a soul companion through this lifetime and beyond.

To Marie, I express heartfelt gratitude for being the Iconic Amazing
Woman you are—a steadfast pillar of support, kindness, and
love. I am truly honored and grateful for your radiant presence
that makes the world a better place.

~Sandra Girouard

Chapter 7

The Courage to Embrace All of Me

The divine light exists within all of Us!
We are simply in different stage of remembering it…
All walking the path of embracing it.

On this Life Journey of Embracing all of Me,
I Choose to STAND BY ME.
In my highest Self Awareness and Loving Acceptance
I cross the threshold to Self-Love.

Written by Sandra Girouard

Life served me on a silver platter exactly what I needed to transcend self-denial, judgement and abandonment, my ultimate human lesson. I lived a life of abandonment, following me like the plague, right from the womb. I was running after love only to be disappointed over and over, feeling empty and abandoned. Wondering WHY ME… WHY is this happening TO ME. That's until I had the courage to see what this life experience was trying to teach me. I realized it was happening FOR ME and I discovered the core of my suffering: Abandonment… of my Self.

It's in the depth of the abyss of abandonment,
where my own self abandonment resided
that I found the most profound deep true Love… For my Self

For as long as I can remember, I have longed to love and be loved!

Children want to be doctors, firemen, teachers... when they grow up. My dream was to be in a loving relationship. Hoping for the prince charming to sweep me away from this childhood of loneliness, abandonment, and emptiness, waiting for time to go by. I couldn't wait to be an adult to finally be with the love of my life.

I felt abandoned all my life. I had the privilege to have two mothers, unfortunately not nurturing, emotionally present nor affectionate. I needed so much to be loved. I remember being 3-4 years old trying to comfort my older brother who was crying. I was trying to love him and be loved only to feel rejection and abandonment.

I replicate the same dynamic in most of my relationships. I truly believed I deeply loved all my boyfriends... yet again, I wasn't loved back. Heartbreak after heartbreak. Until I got the wakeup call....

Almost a lifetime it took for me to see the truth. People can't give what they don't have, it had nothing to do with me and there was nothing wrong with me.

You can only Love and be Loved to the level of your Self Love

We think it's easier to love others and love them more than ourselves. The truth is my love was selfish. I loved others, mostly subconscious, in hope to be loved. I loved to be loved.

Imagine how devastated I was when I realized, one day, through the most amazing relationship I had, that I didn't truly love him! *How could I not love him?* This was the best relationship of my life. The most deep and profound connection ever.

I really felt I loved him with all my heart. I was in love with the way he made me feel, all the ways he loved me. The way he was present to me, looking at me, touching me, talking to me... I was shocked! It took humility to admit that I am human, that I care for what I get out of a relationship, and to embrace my ego who loved that he loved me. It was a shocking revelation when I realized: Love was mostly conditional to how others made me feel.

My actions were based on receiving love, to fill me because I was empty. And no matter how much he did, it was not fulfilling my emptiness. I can recognize today, that even though he's the most amazing, loving, caring, gentle, generous, and present man, it was not enough. I needed more and more, like a bottomless pit. It was not really sinking in. I didn't believe him! He used to tell me: I wish you would see what I see when I look at you. And I, to respond: *God, I wish I could see what you see!*

My biggest contribution to the destruction of this amazing relationship was that I was not loving myself. I kept expecting it from outside. The truth is, at the time I didn't love my Self. I was in codependence, always needing people's approval through their look, words, or touch to remind me that I'm lovable, and that there's nothing wrong with me. I didn't understand why people ran away. They were fleeing, suffocating. I was pulling, holding on, not realizing what I was doing. I blamed and judged people in my life for abandoning me. In fact, it was just the reflection of my own abandonment. I've abandoned my Self.

This was a breakthrough.

I connected with the part of me who didn't WANT to love myself and take care of myself.

I used to say I can't; I don't know how; I didn't have models, nurturing parents or people in my life that made me feel safe; I really want to, but I can't; I don't know how.

One day somebody challenged me: *Oh really? Don't you feel that you are gentle, kind, supportive and loving towards others?* It hit me! *Oh my God, it's not that I can't love myself. It is that I don't want to. I'm blaming and giving excuses. I want someone else to love me and take care of me.*

Facing this truth gave me the courage to hold space for this vulnerable part of me. Through a 4-hour tantrum, I allowed the victim in me to express and feel deeply the experience of NO, I DON'T WANT TO! That was a turning point.

On this Life Journey of Embracing all of Me,
I Choose to STAND BY ME.
In my highest Self Awareness and Loving Acceptance
I cross the threshold to Self-Love.

Passionate about human evolution, there has always been a strong will inside of me to grow, and a profound desire to unstuck myself that drove me to never give up, even in my own unconscious self-abandonment.

So, I embarked on this life journey of Self Mastery and Self Responsibility to Empower my Self, tapping into the depth of my Self to unlock the Genius inside, igniting my inner power, the power of Embrace, this loving acceptance of all I Am.

This life journey of Self Mastery through self-transformation is about amplifying my self-awareness and activating my highest loving acceptance to discover, understand and alleviate my suffering, forgive, and accept my Self. Ultimately, having the Courage to Embrace all of Me.

Embracing is loving all that I Am: my shadow and my light.

We are everything. We carry all the potentials inside: Patience, impatience, kindness, harshness, honesty, dishonesty... All the potentials exist within us so we can grasp the experience of its full spectrum. At first, we behave, do, and think unconsciously, and when we become aware, we can make conscious choice to shift and/ or cultivate other behaviors, attitudes, beliefs. Therefore, our best ally in any transformational, growing process is mindfulness.

Mindfulness is an acknowledgement, judgment free of what is. Without analyzing or labeling as good or bad, right or wrong, no push or pull. When there's no judgment, there is no need to fight, flight, resist or push away. Just an awareness of what is. Cultivating mindfulness helped me discover my Self so I could embrace all that I Am.

How can I embrace other's shadow, darkness,
and flaws if I cannot embrace my own?

Through others I can see the reflection of my own self judgement of the parts of me, conscious or not: the incompetent, childish, insecure, aggressive, codependent, irresponsible, liar, as well as the confident, strong, kind, generous, loving, courageous one. We all have the potential to kill, rob and love. The potentials are there. We might not act on it or maybe we do.

Mindfulness is an invitation to become conscious of it and embrace it, to grasp the wisdom of the experience and become the best conscious version of ourselves. From our soul's perspective, there's no right or wrong, there's only experiences. We are learning and becoming wiser through the experiences. We learn what pain is and what love is. At the core of all the hurtful and painful behavior is the profound desire to be loved.

Life is the ultimate Research & Development Love Lab!

Being aware and having the willingness to see myself just as I am helped me dive into the courage to face my shadow. I stopped blaming outside, and started taking ownership for myself, recognizing I am responsible for my experience, my story, what happens FOR me. Once I embraced the victim in me wanting to be saved and loved, I could let go of the victimhood and start to stand by ME, in integrity.

I cross the threshold of fear, blame, judgment, shame, guilt,
and I step into humility, courage, integrity, responsibility, freedom.

On the path of self-discovery, I found spirituality, where I start expanding my consciousness... deepening my connection with my whole self... unifying the Human, the Soul and the Divine within.

I discovered emotional integration, the practice of embracing all. It's about intentionally dropping into our subconscious mind and sitting at the bottom of darkness, suffering, as well as intentionally dropping into Primordial Joy and Love from within.

I learned to hold a loving and caring space for myself and create a sense of safety inside.

That gave me the foundation to courageously dive at the bottom of my abyss, moving through the darkness, embracing everything deep inside instead of fighting, resisting reacting and rejecting.

It starts with admitting and feeling. The more I felt, the more it dissolved. The more it dissolved, the less power it had over my mind and my body.

It is by looking at myself, lifting the veil to see the truth, observing my ego's mechanic that I was able to eradicate these false conceptions, which are the true roots of suffering. It's through finding their source that I could grasp, understand its nature, and finally free myself.

Let Everything Be... Everything Flow... Everything Go

I released all the heartbreaks, the feeling of rejection and repressed sense of abandonment. I breathe, inhabit, feel, observe, conscious of the drama, embracing without trying to explain it, forgive it, mourn it, heal it. Just giving myself the right to feel the emptiness, the loss. Naturally when our mind is ready, forgiveness happens, healing happens.

Cultivating humility amplifies forgiveness and nurture gratitude.
Everything we resist persists!

I was living my life always in fear of rejection and abandonment, feeling insecure and trying to control everything. I was doing so much, trying, forcing. What should I do? What's wrong with me? What do I need to do? ... until I realized I had nothing to do, simply Be, allowing, surrender.

Surrender means surrendering to the abandonment. Letting go of the control. Because at the bottom of this hole within me, there is unity.

The power of Unity is at the core of Abandonment.

Abandonment allows us to let go of all the walls that makes us believe that we're separated. Where we don't feel our soul or God. Where we feel alone.

It's a long process of dissolution of the separation, of the illusion of separation. It's about believing less and less in the illusion. To do so, I needed to drop into the unknown, in total humility, faith and compassion.

When I embraced abandonment, loneliness disappeared.
In oneness, there is only one consciousness in the universe.
The process hurts but when I finally accept abandonment,
I gain its power: A Joyful Unity!

Being mindful of my self-abandonment started the process of shifting from self-rejection to Self-love. Once I've seen, acknowledged, and embraced the needy inner child that didn't want to grow up, something shifted inside. Somehow, I started to grow up, evolving into a more mature adult, giving myself attention, acknowledgement, validation, listening and comforting myself.

Embrace the depth of your Shadow
and you will have found Self Love.

Spiritual practices provided the foundation to strengthen and amplify my connection with my Higher Self. I learned to reach inside, to feel and connect with the Divine power and the Divine wisdom that I am, to trust life and the divine.

FINALLY, I WASN'T FEELING ALONE ANYMORE!
I was unifying my Divine Self.

I connected to my Soul and started elevating my consciousness. I began to look at myself from within, tapping into the wise Me that trusts life... the part of me that knows how to be happy and free. Feeling grateful for my life, my heart transforms into an expression of pure love and higher consciousness.

How wonderful and precious it is to be conscious!

The Heart is the doorway to the soul. The doorway to feel the experience, to observe judgment free and allowing the experience to teach me... the wisdom.

In our heart lives joy and love. In our heart also lives suffering. Through our heart, we can connect to the darkness and release the suffering, understanding the wisdom and rise, and we can tune into Love and Joy, these states being always within Our Self.

I learned to move from my head to my heart, bringing my attention back into my heart. I was in my head, constantly thinking, analyzing, justifying, rationalizing my life instead of feeling, because in my heart it was too painful.

I developed the reflex to go into my heart to connect with my feelings, my states of being. Because only then can I make wise conscious choice. I can be anything. I can do anything. I can think anything. I can choose, knowing that all is experienced to help me grow, evolve, and expand.

The heart is the key.
Trusting my heart,
being guided through my heart.
Leading my life from my heart:
Talk, feel, act, teach, guide,
and support through my heart.

Let's hang out in the heart!
So much self-denial slowly dissolving into self-awareness.
Accessing the nectar of love within!

Loving my shadow was hard, maybe as hard as loving the light that I am.

I remembered:

We all are unique in our own essence.
We are all a piece of God, a specific flavor of the whole,
like a drop of the ocean.
God's emancipating, being aware of itself, of all it can be,
through each drop of God that we are,
Experiencing all the potential combinations and interactions.

While discovering my Self, I started to recognize my own beauty, my essence, my uniqueness. Understanding that embracing my essence was not taking away anything from others as it's unique. Just like recognizing the power, the beauty, the light in others didn't take away anything from me.

Compassion is embracing the power of all Souls to co-create their experience, recognizing the struggle we experience in our evolution, and a loving compassion for all our humanity. It is also recognizing that each one of us is a being of light, that we all are love and divine, without feeling threatened by others. I don't need to dim my light, so you don't feel inferior, nor do you need dim your light, so I don't feel inferior. We all are part of this masterpiece of colors, all the different shades of the infinite possibility of colors the divine can be!

One day, in my journey of loving my Self, I experienced my own soul touch, my gift. I used to be a massage therapist, aware of the pure love flowing through my touch, yet disappointed to never find someone with the same touch and not able to touch myself the same way. Finally, I was able to give it to myself. I felt it. I had this eureka moment realizing that nobody could give me that. Not in my mind, but in my soul, I grasped that wisdom. I started to experience being the giver and the receiver. I was able to feel that love as a receiver, understanding that I was allowing myself to be touched by the Divine within, this power of love, my soul Touch.

One day, in the words of Alana Fairchild, I found my calling to co-create a world of Love:

Lion of Love
A leader of the new way of love upon this sacred earth,
to lead with my heart,
roaring love from the dept of my soul,
with compassion and tenacious devotion
to the cause of the quest of the human soul.
TOGETHER, with love, we claim divine victory.
We are Love. We are light. We are Divine Power.

I am honored to be a vessel, in service to the expansion of the Unified Self… deepening the connection with my whole self… the human, the soul, and the Divine within.

But at the same time, I also questioned myself, *"How can I be a lion of love when I distrust and deny myself?"* There must be a mistake.

The wisdom I found: You can only truly see and recognize light in the darkness. You cannot become an amazing being! You must remember you already are one! You do not become a diamond. You just remove all the dirt that covers it!

The divine light is within all of Us!
We are just in different stage of remembering it...
All walking the path of embracing it.

Also, I considered myself way too selfish and egocentric, to be in service of LOVE.

One day after watching a movie where a safety diver dies in service to another free diver, I had an 'aha' moment, a shift in my perspective. At first, I believed that I hadn't touched and contributed much to the world like he did with his tenacious devotion to others. And then it hit me! *I inspire people to have this tenacious devotion to the Self.*

Doing whatever it takes to support our Self
is the best way to support others.
Me loving all of me inspires you to love all of you!

My path, my gift is to live a life dedicated to the grown of consciousness and opening the doorway. I will walk in the abyss with you. And provide a safe space through the uncomfortable process of looking inside and facing your shadow and the beauty of your own soul. I will guide you to create and hold that safe space for your Self to dive in and bring to light what is in the dark... to see your triggers... to befriend your ego and understand your ego mechanisms... to grasp the wisdom and make wiser conscious choices and decisions. Most of all... to be better equipped to move through emotional discomfort instead of being paralyzed by it and overwhelmed by your experiences... to become the observer as opposed to the victim of life, people, situation, emotions... To ignite the courage to be present to your Self... to embrace your unified Self... to find Inner Peace.

It's through the doorway of courage that we begin...
That's the threshold where we cross from fear to self-love.

109

Fear freezes us and keeps us stuck. Fear to be judged and abandoned, fear of being vulnerable... fear of seeing ourselves truly and completely. My own personal difficulty about sitting in fear was my resistance to it...I DIDN'T WANT to feel the fear. I was only seeing it as a signal to run away.

Choosing to embrace fear as an ally
is the key to igniting inner courage.

Being willing to look at fear has led me to a new inner dialogue where fear has become my ally pointing me into the courage to Be...

When walking through fear and deepen your presence to it, you step into your courageous self, releasing the obstacles, allowing the wisdom to be revealed and the gift of unfolding what you are truly...

Empowered to dare to BeYoutiFul,
with the courage to Embrace all of you!

Through the courage of being vulnerable, I realized that vulnerability is my strength, the source of my power to transform. I can let go of what no longer serves me, with all my heart, in complete forgiveness and acceptance, and rejoice by tuning in and radiating the primordial Joy and Love within.

Trusting, surrendering, and embracing my shadow set me free from the walls and chains... AND love surfaced, radiating, expanding inside out. It was right there, hidden in the dept of my suffering.

It's through humility, integrity, strength, and courage that I took responsibility for my life. Be discovering my Soul Esteem, my essence, my own unique flavor I am free to Embrace my Self fully, the magnificent, powerful, fascinating, beautiful being I Am.

Personal growth and spiritual practice are essential for our ongoing growth and evolution, to expand our consciousness, understand our Self, and Embrace our Unified Self – Human/Soul/Divine.

Let's co-create this new way of love. Let's hang out in our Heart.

Let's inspire each other to:

Stand in our Sacred Authority and High Integrity
Align and anchor in our Soul Esteem
Embracing our whole Self
Daring to BeYoutiFul
Recognizing and embracing that
We are Light. We are Love. We are Divine Power

Opening the Possibilities to live a mindful, meaningful, joyful life
with more Depth, Authenticity, Integrity, and Love!
Connected to this endless flow of our life force, Divine Energy.

About Sandra Girouard

Your sacred Ally, Soul Touch Mentor, Spiritual and Personal Growth Guide in service to awakening your highest Self-Awareness and Loving Acceptance to Embrace all of Your Self, opening the doorway of living a Mindful, Meaningful, Joyful Life with more Depth, Authenticity, Integrity, and Love.

Passionate about Human Evolution, Sandra is committed to support you to ignite your Courageous Self, crossing the threshold from Fear to Self-Love, and empowering you to Dare to BeYoutiFul.

For over 20 years she has served as a respected training coach in Optimal health and wellness, resiliency, and human skill development. Sandra works closely with corporations to create cultures that provide leadership strategies and support to manage priorities based on optimal energy, bringing teams to their optimal functioning and to achieve their full potential.

She also assists people living an Optimal balanced life through the awakening of becoming more physically energized, emotionally connected, mentally focused, and spiritually aligned.

Creator of *Building Resilience, Mastery of the Heart* and *Optimal Energy Lifestyle* programs, her work has touched multi-thousands of lives… both professionally and personally… giving way to building a culture of leading with the heart, inspiring an expanded consciousness and self-transcendence.

For more information about Sandra Girouard and her work visit:

www.SoulTouch.com

Or Facebook where there are links to my other pages:

https://www.facebook.com/sandra.girouard.7/

LinkedIn:
https://www.linkedin.com/in/sandra-girouard-66b00540/

This chapter is dedicated to my mom, Ruth Aileen Brunner.

She was intelligent and capable and grew up when women only aspired to be housewives. Her talent was writing; she would have been a fantastic writer, but was stuck in writing our local paper. She was intelligent, funny, and witty.

I know she wanted more for herself because she always wanted to be and dancer and couldn't, so that became my legacy.

I became what she always wanted to be. I loved the dance world and all that I learned from those years. I have only recently embodied my mom's feelings about her body and life. She had always want to change her body, work on her arms and lose weight; nothing clicked for her.

My mother inspired my work with women and my commitment to deep listening to what our bodies are telling us. She has influcnced my love of writing and my love of people.

She is whom I think about when I get a note or a question from women across the globe who want to feel better in their bodies and live a pain-free life.

Thank you, and love you, Mom.

~Conni Ponturo

Chapter 8

The Wave of The New Self-Healer

"Our natural abilities to sense and to know our bodies…
to be receptive to the subtle, finer messages of the body…
to recognize and honor what the body is
saying and speaking…
that's where true inner healing begins."

Written by Conni Ponturo

It wasn't too many years ago that the term INNER HEALER would be a surprising use of words.

Maybe it still is?

Our capacities to heal… today go well beyond what we may have expected or even found acceptable in years past.

So, we begin by asking ourselves:

What is it to be an INNER HEALER, and why are we being called to become one now?

The Healer archetype seeks to restore balance or create
growth in an individual, community, or organization.
The work manifests through different modalities.

The mission is to raise awareness, connect and transform.
An Intuitive Healer guides and establishes the path
and seeks unity of mind, body, and spirituality.

Awakening Your Inner Healer

How can we elevate the quality of our self-healing?

As someone who teaches clients about self-healing, I have been in a personal rut. I have felt disconnected and lost lately… shedding my old skin so that a newer perspective and person can emerge feels right. It is a challenging transition for me. I feel like I am wearing new clothes or a different size, so everything within me feels foreign. I am digging into my teaching to help me through this; this is what I have discovered about my journey.

You get to choose the journey you are on. It isn't up to anyone else.

Your journey of discovery might be one day or over years, and all of it is valid.

We haven't been trained to become good listeners, so you can start by reviewing these questions.

I started by asking myself some questions I needed to be truthful about.

Do I feel worthy?

Do I know enough about what my body needs to help myself grow and change?

Do I feel worthy enough to devote time to my body? Does that feel selfish to me?

Can I make myself the most critical person in my life?

In answering these questions in my journal, I decided to be easy and tender with myself instead of being strong. I decided to ask myself to do 10 minutes of a task if it felt hard. This felt doable. I reached for easy and fun things to do each day and embraced each day with a newfound hope of how I wanted to feel in my body. I went for walks in nature. I spent more time breathing into any discomfort I felt in my body. I moved my body with fascia-inspired somatic movements that felt good, even if it was only 10 minutes every day. The only feeling I wanted to lean into was being happy and safe where I was, nothing more. I released my attachment to any outcome.

How can we make peace with ourselves?

How can we make peace with our self-worth and self-value... become kinder in our conversations about our bodies and our devotion to care of our bodies?

When I say devotion, I don't mean going to the gym for endless hours or starving your body to be thinner. I mean true devotion.

The definition of devotion means "feeling strong or genuine affection, dedication," a prayer."

We can feel devotion to our children, grandchildren, careers, and partners, but we rarely allow ourselves to feel devotion to ourselves fully and deeply. If you live in chronic pain or want to change your body for some reason, you must become devoted to yourself and your beautiful body above all else.

I am reframing your pain to be honored as a gift instead of an annoyance. That means doing the hard work sometimes and sometimes not doing anything.

Here is a quote that I want you to copy and post somewhere so you can see it often.

"I can do hard things."

I have this on the wall in my studio, and when someone complains about something being too hard, I point to this quote by Glennon

Doyle. Not feeling good about things…well, that can be challenging. But, with trust and self-care, we can do them.

We are so much more capable than we allow ourselves to be.

This is because we have a reptilian brain that often stops us. As humans, we are wired for the negative and are always looking for danger. This has served us as we lived thousands of years ago, but today, we need to override those thoughts to make the necessary changes in self-care. Otherwise, we spin our wheels and repeatedly do the same destructive behaviors.

Let's simultaneously be brave and gentle as we break the cycle of neglecting our bodies and leaning into how we want to feel.

What vision do you want, and how do you want to feel and look in your body?

What is self-healing? And how can we awaken our inner healer and deep intuition?

- Self-healing is the process of healing or discovering what one needs to promote recovery in the body… process chronic pain in the body… place yourself at the top of the list of importance.

- Put supreme value into taking care of your body.

- Create positive emotions that will release the 'happy hormones,' elevating your feelings about your life.

- When you break a bone, the body rushes quickly, beginning the healing. The body instinctively knows. When you make yourself conscious of the healing your body asks for, you become your body's own emergency line.

- Create guidelines and methods to help you become more cognitive, highly perceptive, and intuitive where you weren't before.

- Listen to your soul... amplify the voice of the soul... you begin to listen to your true nature.

- It is about dropping into your body and listening to your true nature; the voice of your soul can be heard. It's held in the body, in the muscles. Self-compassion and self-awareness... these move you toward becoming a self-healing human.

- When you become a self-healer, self-responsibility takes place... taking responsible action... life is happening for you and not to you. Begin by seeing your pain as the gift that it is.

- Surrender to who you are and who you want to become. *How do you want to live in your body... how do you want to function in the world?*

What is your intuition?

You know the feeling. It's a 'knowing' or a gentle nudge that something is off, extraordinary, or needs our attention. It's typically subtle, so we often miss or discount it.

Researchers at Leeds University concluded that intuition is an authentic psychological process where the brain uses past experiences and cues from the self and the environment to decide. The decision happens so quickly that it doesn't register on a conscious level.

Intuition is the way the subconscious mind communicates with the conscious mind. The information in our brains that gives us that feeling or inner knowing is absolute. But how the information comes together happens outside our conscious awareness, so it can be hard to trust or listen to.

Intuition is using your 6ᵗʰ sense to care for and love your body.

Each of us comes into the world 100 percent intuitive; It is just a matter of reclaiming your birthright. To do that, you must get out of your way to strip away the thoughts and things that are blocking, distracting, diffusing, suppressing, and diminishing the natural dance of your intuition.

So why is your intuition important, and what does it do with self-healing?

- To become the most authentic version of yourself, to see who you are.
- To truly listen to who you want to become and to become present.
- The highest purpose of intuition is to serve your highest self and to listen deeply to the longing of your heart, which will heal and serve your body at its deepest level.

Have you considered intuition one of your most important life skills?

Image the ease when you allow your deeper knowing to be your greatest asset.

Have you ever said this?

"I have a gut feeling about that person; I just know it in my body.

I feel something here. I know that person; I've been to this place before."

These are all examples of our intuition. Most of us don't trust our feelings or more profound knowing, but when we do, we usually say, *"I knew that, or I felt that. Why didn't I listen to myself?"*

So, we do know, but we don't trust our more profound knowing. It is scary, and what if we are wrong? That feeling of being wrong stops us daily. What if we reframe that into thinking of our mistakes as stepping-stones to our greatest truth?

The way to the truth about our inner world is through our mistakes. We can embrace our mistakes or missteps to move quicker in healing.

We have not been guided or allowed to rely on our deeper knowing in society. It's an undervalued trait. In contrast, I have allowed my instinct and intuition to be the cornerstone of my teaching and training. Both are priceless to growing my business. Both allow me to greet my clients in an environment where they simultaneously feel seen and hopeful.

Imagine: There are answers within you… a capacity to step into rhythm with what your body is speaking. But first, we must accept and understand the true capacities of our intuitive abilities.

There are four avenues of your intuition. Some are stronger within you than others.

1. Clairaudience: The ability to hear what isn't audible in our outer world.
2. Clairvoyance: The ability to see possibilities and potential events in the future.
3. Clairsentience: The ability to tap into someone's feelings.
4. Claircognizance: The ability to perceive situations without knowing why.

Your intuition can be seen as the voice of inner guidance talking to you. It speaks up occasionally, and we all have different abilities regarding what shows up for us. The more we trust, the stronger it gets, just like the muscles in our bodies. That's why we train our muscles to support us when needed. It is the same with our intuition;

the more we use it and trust it to be accurate, the better listener we become… hearing our wants and desires.

For hundreds of years, using our instincts has been considered harmful, inferior to science, and maybe even witchcraft. But today, this inner knowing has much validity. It is the brain's way to shortcut the system with memories and knowledge you have acquired. So now, it is beginning to be valued in the workplace. This is the key that will help you unlock the resistance in your body and allow you to achieve a better overall change.

How can we develop a deeper connection to our instincts?

Start slow and allow yourself to be a beginner.

Follow your enthusiasm for things.

Seek answers and ask questions in your sleep.

Take an intuitive walk or go from impulse-to-impulse activity for a day.

Make using a journal part of your daily activity. Even 5- 10 minutes is valuable.

Use better words that you say about your body and your life and begin to see how things around you change as you use more uplifting words. *"I am good with electronics. I am becoming a better listener. I am becoming more assertive in my body every day and every way."* Start by leaning into already being where you want to end up. As if it already exists. That way, your mind can believe it to be true.

Ask yourself daily, *"How do I feel today?"* Listen for the answer.

Most people's first response will always be, *"I don't know."* I think it is a fear of not wanting to be wrong about the answer, but there is no right or wrong in the body. So, after each experience or exercise, ask, *"How do I feel when doing this?"*

You can use the following methods to begin deepening trust in yourself.

1. <u>Meditate:</u> Spend 5-10 minutes in silence, listening to beautiful music or focusing on breathing. If this feels hard, set your alarm for 3 minutes and focus on slowly taking a deep breath in and blowing out.

2. <u>Practice mindfulness:</u> Slow down and be in the moment of your activity. Eat without looking at your phone. Taste and be in the moment of eating. Stroll and look at all the trees and nature around you. Drive with an awareness of what is around you. Take a breath in, and slowly exhale. Allow your shoulders to relax.

3. <u>Check in with your body:</u> When you wake up every morning before you get out of bed, say thank you. Then, take a quick scan of your feelings without any judgment. Practice this same Thank you to your body before you fall asleep.

4. <u>Allow yourself to feel:</u> Emotions can come and go in our bodies every day. Try to feel whatever shows up at any moment. We can get through our emotions faster without judging and leaning into the feeling. Emotions are energy in motion, so let them move through you.

5. <u>Let yourself daydream:</u> When I was little, I would lie on the grass and look up at the clouds, giggle, and dream with my girlfriend for hours. We stop doing that as adults, and we stop dreaming. Is there something you have been dreaming of? Maybe it's time to step into a bigger vision of your dream.

6. <u>Try things on.</u> Try a new outfit, a different exercise class, a new shade of lipstick, a new way home, take another

course, or read another book you don't usually read. Who else can you be in your life?

7. <u>Pay attention to serendipity:</u> Crazy coincidences happen constantly, but we rarely pay attention to them. When we do, we can find connections. Pay attention, and you will notice more of them.

8. <u>Notice other people's energy:</u> You want to be aware of the energy you are around. You have people who feel excellent to be around, and you always feel good when you leave them. And the contrast is true, as well. You may also have people who tend to make you feel bad about yourself when you are around them. Cut those people from your life. Pay acute attention to how your body feels around these people.

We all have intuition, and each of us can tap into our intuition to help us reach our most genuine potential. It's up to us whether we choose to listen. You can use the methods here to deepen trust in your intuition and elevate your innate self-healing power.

Choose one method and start practicing it for a week. Keep notes in your journal of hunches, nudges, or feelings you experience throughout the week. Then, at the end of the week, read over your experiences and see if anything came true for you.

What happened when you followed a nudge?

What happened when you ignored a knowing?

Write about all your experiences to build self-awareness and deepen trust in your intuition. The more you trust yourself, the more your intuition will show up.

Putting it all together, awaking the power of the SEM Method...

As a teacher, I've invested years in understanding the body's potent and profound healing capacities. Along the way, I've developed a collection of proven techniques that have helped my clients heal and begin to feel more in control of their lives — giving them peace of mind and feeling hopeful again and in control of their chronic pain.

Putting this all together, I created a new system that works excellently throughout my teachings. I call it THE SEM METHOD. SEM is an acronym for SAFETY. ENERGY. MOBILIZE. Through my years of working with clients, I've found safety, energy, and the ability to mobilize are the foundation of our natural abilities to sense and to know our bodies... to be receptive to the subtle, finer messages of the body... to recognize and honor what the body is saying and speaking... and that's where true inner healing begins.

Sometimes, on our journey of self-healing, we get locked into what we feel we don't have in our lives. Our body has been talking to us on a deep level, but we can't hear it. These proven techniques help open the communication in the body so you can listen to what your body has been trying to tell you all along.

S: *Safety.* We create safety before we can do anything with our bodies; we must feel safe in our environment and our bodies. Next, we strengthen the body by working with weights body weight and building core strength to train the entire body.

E: *Energy.* We breathe into our bodies the energy we need to feel so that our bodies can feel alive. Creating I Am statements about how we want to feel and live in our bodies. Then, we engage in deep rest restoration and breathwork to restore the body.

M: *Mobilize.* Moving the body with fascia-inspired movements allows the joints and muscles to feel their best.

To change our bodies or rather to inspire ourselves to take inspired steps to learn new habits that will allow us to live in a vibrant and more joyful body takes time. Your time is well worth it and can elevate how you feel daily.

And finally, to encourage you along your own unique journey of becoming a self-healer… to anchor your dedication… to remember your inner power… here is a collection of I AM STATEMENTS OF INTENTION.

As you speak each short statement, consider it a gentle nudge to continue awakening and deepening your relationship with your Inner Healer. Allow these statements to be your new truth, even if it feels hard.

Breathe into each statement.

1. I am brave.

2. I am happy to be here.

3. I am always learning.

4. I am an intelligent being.

5. I am proud of who I am.

6. I am happy.

7. I am responsible.

8. I am not in a race; there is plenty of time.

9. I am strong.

10. I am going to get through this.

11. I am unique.

12. I am patient.

13. I am worthy.

14. I am loveable.

15. I am fun.

16. I am creative.

17. I am trustworthy.

18. I am a survivor.

19. I am loved.

20. I am "me".

And this collection of STATEMENTS OF INTENTION is only the beginning. Create your own I AM statement. Feel the energy of your words. Infuse them with certainty, speaking in the present tense and positive.

May the techniques I've provided you with become part of your healing toolbox. Now, it is up to you to pick one or two techniques to experiment with. Keep it simple. Watch the magic appear in your body and your life. Remember, my amazing woman friend, you are the inner healer. Trust in your ability. Open to new possibilities. Allow a new vision to emerge, a radiant potential to live pain-free.

About Conni Ponturo

Respected as a knowledgeable and compassionate teacher by hundreds of clients and students, Conni Ponturo's holistic approach to somatic movement, breath, and intuitive inner healing meets you where you are on your healing journey.

She teaches that you can empower your ability to ignite your inner-healing capacities, reduce pain, increase body strength, remain balanced, and mitigate stress by becoming more aware of what your body is communicating through intuitive insight, somatic awareness, meditation, and fascia-inspired movement techniques. Conni holds multiple certifications from the *Pilates Method Alliance, Balanced Body,* and *Physical Mind Institute and is a certified fascial fitness teacher.* She is a certified breast cancer exercise specialist with the Pink Ribbon Program and an advanced breathwork practitioner with Pause Breathwork.

Her book *Listen: Watch What You Say Your Body Is Listening.* is a bestseller on Amazon. Download her app *Absolutely Grounded* for free videos to get you moving and feeling good in your body.

For more information about Conni Ponturo and her work, visit www.absolutelygrounded.com

AMAZING WOMAN

DIVINE INSIGHTS

Divine Insight

The time has come to embrace a new level of freedom.
As more and more women access their true power as
expressed through the Divine Feminine,
our voice will rise as a joyful expression of
caring and cooperation, creativity, and true confidence.

Roby Lynn Chevance

We are now living in the exciting time of the divine feminine RISING and the core dynamic of divine feminine is the energetic of RECEIVING. When we cultivate our consciousness to own our gifts, to claim our just compensation, to embrace the benefits that are realized when we trust and cooperate with the greater good, then we are living as divine feminine. We then embrace each other, support each other, and come together in a grand coalescence of expanded good from a place of peace, poise, trust, and abundance. This is the magic of woman: receiving, having, BEING the gifts of life and then joyfully multiplying them to something greater that benefits all.

This is the call to rise we are answering — opening ourselves to let others in and learning to work in cooperation and inclusion. The goodness of life multiplies exponentially through the coming together of like minds in co-creating greater outcomes that benefit a greater number of people.

This requires us to claim our wholeness, our brilliance, our creativity, and our power. We have nothing to prove and everything to express. There is nothing to sacrifice and everything to gain. We know there is greater power in numbers, and we do not have to do it all ourselves. This knowledge infuses into our relationship with the very activity of how life works. We are now questioning old paradigms about how things need to be accomplished and when we ask a question, it automatically places us in the position of receiving an answer!

And when we allow ourselves to listen and receive, multiple possibilities will arise and cause the heavy scales of false belief and limitation to fall away from our thinking, revealing the true nature of the all-possibility that is always ever present and available for us. When we turn away from a world that has told us we cannot have the joy of our desires, when we untether our soul from the judgments and conclusions of our conditioned world, and give more credibility to the "YES!" within us, to all that we are willing to allow, we dwell in a life that is paradise on earth—whether we are taking out the trash or saving a rain forest.

It is in mastering the microcosm of our own lives that we take our rightful place as the midwives of the Age of Enlightenment and co-create a new macrocosm of cooperation within our world. This is how we are creating our divine legacy that will reach further than we ever imagined.

FEMININE PROSPERITY PRACTICE

I believe in the power of asking questions. Here are some questions I ask that invite Divine Cooperation from the Universe and keep me in the energetic of receiving:

I wonder where can I be the greatest contribution on the planet?

I wonder who can I add to my team/life/staff that will expand the greater good beyond anything I could ever imagine?

What is right about me/this that I am not seeing?

I wonder how this can work out better than I ever could imagine?

What would it take for me to wake up every morning, feeling as if I had to pinch myself because I could not believe my life was real?

About Roby Lynn Chevance

Minister, teacher, inspirational speaker, and psychic medium; Roby Lynn Chevance inspires people to live an ease filled life by teaching them the creative power of asking questions, the accuracy of their own intuitive abilities, and the awareness of energy and using it to work for them.

She has a profound ability to trust the Infinite Unseen Realm to manifest in delightful and miraculous ways and believes our mission is to create a world that works for everyone.

For more information about Roby Lynn Chevance and her work visit www.RobyLynn.com

Divine Insight

I escape any cages that life circumstances bring me.
I dismantle them, and from their broken pieces
create a beautiful masterpiece.

Carol Patricia Koppelman

Having lived nearly 70 years on this beautiful earth, I've gained wisdom – mostly through the practice of what NOT to do. Making mistakes is where our journey teaches us the best lessons. A good, but rather chaotic upbringing made me resilient, but also left me with a hypervigilant, perfectionistic spirit. That spirit certainly served me in chaotic corporate environments, and by the time I left corporate life, I had achieved all my career goals, including a six-figure salary — the same salary my male colleagues were making. However, that spirit did not make my personal life calm or secure. I drank and partied too much in youth, seeking solace and what I perceived as love in shallow and emotionally catastrophic love affairs, one of which culminated in a ten-year marriage to an emotionally abuse alcoholic, living in emotional, physical, and financial scarcity.

My transformation began when I returned to a church that focused on love instead of doctrine and providentially met a light being who showed me the path where I could live in abundance and not fear, gratitude instead of despair. Both these choices transformed my life completely. When she retired, I found another light being who encourages me to continue down that path. I believe that I manifested my second husband, who is truly the love of my life. The life I imagined is the life I'm living now, and I'm consistently updating my vision for here and now and for the future. I don't look back, I look forward. We really do only have today.

I believe that all women are iconic – just be BEING. We are intrinsically gifted with tremendous intuition, unique survival skills from our ancestors. To continue to refine those iconic qualities, we simply allow ourselves to grow and evolve.

FEMININE PROSPERITY PRACTICE

Breath — in and out and in and out, until you are in a place of gratitude, without fear or stress. Focus on your dreams, your wishes, your vision. Be undeterred by the noise of the world, the noise of your problems, the noise of darkness. Believe God's truth — love and live in and with an abundance reality. Problems will come, but when we focus on what's true — life will reveal the answers.

About Carol Koppelman

Carol Patricia Koppelman is the best-selling author of *Do the Necessary, Let the Rest Go to Hell.*

Additionally, she is a featured contributor to multiple International Bestsellers.

As a Branch Director for Park Lane Jewelry, Carol styles women with beautiful jewelry, emphasizing their intrinsic beauty.

Her website is

parklanejewelry.com/rep/carolkoppelman.

She is also CEO of CPK Solutions, LLC, an Arizona-based business. Her website is cpksolutions.com.

Divine Insight

*Every day I find I'm rediscovering myself in novel ways
and cultivating a deeper relationship with who I am.*

Debra Shoults Bettendorf

In the heat-drenched embrace of July 2022, Southeastern Belize beckoned with its azure waters and tranquil shores. A day etched in my memory began with a pilgrimage to the Xunantunich Mayan Ruins. Amidst the ancient stones and the hum of archaeologists meticulously unearthing history, I felt a resonance—an unexpected chord struck deep within my soul.

Our journey then led us deeper into Belize's heart, to the mystical embrace of a river that flowed beneath the towering Belize mountains, and preparation for a tubing adventure. Donning helmets crowned with headlights, we ventured into an abyss, where daylight surrendered to enveloping darkness.

Everywhere my headlight touched were walls adorned with glistening formations, resembling nature's own cathedral of crystal and stone. The silence was palpable, punctuated only by the gentle cadence of dripping water and the distant serenade of a waterfall. Amidst this subterranean serenity, a profound introspection enveloped me, prompting a heartfelt dialogue with the Divine.

Seeking clarity amidst life's natural wonders, I turned to God, articulating my yearnings for guidance. Inside my mind I asked for a sign. Initially, I sought validation through the familiar embrace of the number 11, a recurring motif in my life's journey. My aspirations shifted and I recalibrated my request, seeking the presence of a dragonfly, a symbol of transformation and spiritual awakening. Yet, in a whimsical twist of intuition, I invoked a seemingly random sign — a lost shoe, a playful testament to the unpredictable nature

139

of divine communication. As I emerged from the subterranean experience, I was greeted by a kaleidoscope of dragonflies adorning the sky and then I looked down and two dragonflies alighted upon my wrist, forming an unmistakable silhouette of the number 11, a profound sense of connection enveloped me — a divine affirmation that sounded deep down in my soul. I then giggled to myself and appreciated the signs but silently said, "But I changed my mind from the number 11 and the dragonfly and firmly decided on seeing a lost shoe." We finished our float and exited the cool water, holding our tubes and walking single file up wooden steps. I then heard my husband who was in front of me say, "Ha, look at that, a lost shoe!" A yell of some sort escaped my body and he turned to ask me what was wrong. I told him I would tell him later.

In the ensuing silence, enveloped by the rhythmic cadence of our journey back, I remained immersed in contemplation, awestruck by the intricate dance of signs and symbols orchestrated by the Divine, reaffirming my path, and fostering a deeper communion with the universe.

Since July 11, 2022, an event titled, *"The Number 11, The Dragonfly, and The Lost Shoe"* has remained etched in my memory, echoing in my thoughts every single day. Waves of both disbelief and comfort washed over me, creating a perplexing yet oddly soothing blend of emotions. It was as though the universe whispered secrets directly into my soul.

The signs I had fervently sought manifested in the most wondrous manner imaginable. This wasn't mere coincidence; it felt like a divine gift bestowed upon me. For a prolonged period, I chose silence, holding this profound experience close to my heart, shielding it from the external world. It became my sanctuary — a realm of reflection, wonder, and deep contemplation.

But what emotions surface now, over a year later? A recent epiphany illuminated the true essence of that transformative moment. My initial inquiry to the cosmos was framed as, "God, reveal the significance of that experience. Illuminate the lessons it intended to impart." At the core of this quest lay a more profound, introspective question: Was I genuinely deserving of pursuing my loftiest aspirations?

While I acknowledged the divine signals as affirmations of my chosen path, a subtle undercurrent of doubt lingered — questioning my inherent worthiness of those grand dreams. Today, I confront this internal dialogue with unabashed honesty, recognizing the duality of my journey: the quest for purpose and the pursuit of self-worth.

FEMININE PROSPERITY PRACTICE

I find solace in nature. A suggestion I would offer to all is to immerse oneself in the outdoors, allowing your feet to connect with the earth, inhaling deeply, and truly embracing the present moment. The experience has a profound effect on rejuvenating both our minds and bodies.

About Debra Shoults Bettendorf

As a fashion entrepreneur and founder of Studio 11 Style, Debra Shoults Bettendorf is devoted to ensuring every woman feels valued, empowered and 'fabulous within'.

Her strong commitment to female empowerment drives her to cultivate an ever-growing supportive community where women celebrate each other's achievements and embrace their unique strengths. As host of the popular podcast series, FIND IT!, she calls upon her deep empathetic nature to connect with people on a deeply intimate level while providing a platform for voices and views to be shared, fostering open dialogue, personal growth, and mutual respect. Her book, *Find Your Fabulous: Love Yourself on the Inside, Look Great on the Outside* is a blend of heart and soul with a dose of fashion … and is filled with an abundance of positivity, charm, and wit. Debra believes you are never too young or too old to *Find Your Fabulous*.

To learn more about Debra Bettendorf and her work visit: www.findyourfabulous11.com.

Divine Insight

Dream it. Feed that flame burning inside yourself.
Breathe life into it.
Let all the forces of the universe
gather to support you…
*as only **you** are destined*
to birth your gifts and bring them forward.
Doubts? Fear? Do it anyway.

Diane Sova

"What the hell is the matter with you?" "You goddamn idiot!" "Where in hell did you come from? Go back!" "Get your ugly fat ass out of here." Those words, yelled by my father throughout my youth, formed my core beliefs about myself. I did everything to escape – drinking, drugs, sex, living hard to numb out.

In my early 20s, a friend gave me a book that literally changed my life. From *The Dynamic Laws of Prosperity* by Catherine Ponder, I learned that I could change my thinking and change my life. It worked!! To this day, I guard the words I speak and especially those I think. Our thoughts are sacred things, under our control and no one else's.

Overcoming the influences of my early life, I realized that I – and only I – had authority over my own life (and my mind). Curiosity about how far I could go drove me to make choices that served myself both in the outer world and my inner world.

At 19, I gave birth and kept my child, even after being told that I shouldn't because I was too young.

At 29, I opened a business, after being told I shouldn't because I needed a 'real' job.

At 39, I earned my first college degree, after being told there wasn't any reason to get it at my age.

At 49, I moved to Jerusalem, earning another degree while teaching at the University there, after being told it was too dangerous.

At 59, when I was not-so-gently 'retired,' I set off on my own to see the world, after being told I couldn't because I was diabetic, too old to travel alone, it was to risky... blah, blah, blah. I traveled for nearly 5 years straight!

Our world is full of amazing, good people, and I was privileged to meet meany of them. My trust in myself grew. My connection with people who nourished my soul, my connection to source, and my connection to SELF became stronger.

I did it anyway. You can, too. Thoughts and other people's opinions are just that, opinions, not your truth. Every single day is a new opportunity to create yourself. Every person you meet is a new opportunity for connection. We hear that love is everything... I believe that connection is everything. Create your way, *YOUR WAY.*

Focus on what *you* want your world to be and DO IT ANYWAY!

FEMININE PROSPERITY PRACTICE

Two things to help DO IT ANYWAY:

1. When dark feelings of doubt, despair, or anger come upon you, give yourself time to deeply feel that way. Have your own 10-minute pity party or raging rant. When time is up, take a deep breath, recalibrate, and move on to feeling marvelous.

2. When thoughts about a person or event keep repeating, say "Thank you, bye-bye" and let them pass. No need to

let them waste any more of your precious time and energy. It's surprising how many times you might say "Thank you, bye-bye" in one day!

About Diane Sova

Diane's academic studies spanned science and spirit. After earning a degree in Business, she went on to earn a BS in Systems Engineering, then BA degrees in Cultural Anthropology and Comparative Religion.

She later earned her master's degree in Space Operations, and a master's degree in religious studies. These seemingly polar opposites enable her to readily bridge people, cultures, science, and beliefs.

For more information about Diane Sova and her work visit: www. dianesova.com

Divine Insight

A woman of wealth operates
from the spiritual bank of faith and gratitude.
Nurturing the operating system within first
and creating from a foundation of well-being.

Donata De Luca

In my obsession towards achieving financial success, I was STRIPPED NAKED. Stripped naked of my health, my vitality, my beliefs, my habits, my values, my addictions, my relationships, my belongings… even facing my mortality… truly the complete death of my old identity.

I was engulfed in a very dark night of the soul, every part of me felt torn apart, my body hurt, my heart pained. I preferred 'numbing out' instead of feeling deep. My spinning mind was unbearable. A sense of guilt and shame was suffocating. An empty fridge and the shock of facing eviction as a single mother brought me to the ultimate humiliation.

The heaviness of this persona brought me to the final blow… facing my own mortality. Facing mortality initiated me to connect to the wisdom of my body and RISE UP to the wholeness of my divinity, my shadow and my light, the embodiment of my sacred feminine and sacred masculine.

This was my journey of learning what it means to STAND IN MY POWER.

I got radically honest with myself. I became my own coaching client, my own teacher. I took the lead of my life.

There is money and there is wealth… YOU can have both!

147

For me, this was the rebirth of a WOMAN AND WEALTH. It ignited my inner worth to discover my true wealth…my inner riches, my true power.

True wealth is a holistic approach of creating from a foundation of well-being. It's operating from the spiritual bank of faith and gratitude. It's a new relationship with money.

It's a redefinition of success.

My new success formula is:

1) Regulating of the nervous system

2) Self-care and self-love

3) Fulfillment

Redefining success awakened a new rhythm within me… now willing to find the power of SLOW is SEXY. Slow does not mean inaction, procrastination, or confusion. It's a richly empowered connection to the wisdom of our body, regulation of our nervous system, respecting our rhythm.

Energy management versus time management. We have no control over time, but we do have control over our energy. This is a powerful practice that rules out burnout.

Self-care and self-love… they are not only about rest, hot baths, and sleep. Self-care and self-love are becoming radically self-honest with ourselves. It's slowing down, valuing stillness and mindfulness, saying no, setting boundaries… a willingness to ask for what we require and face the tough conversations … it's an observation of our inner dialogue, taking inventory of our values and beliefs… and it is getting intimate with our bank account, evaluating our inner and outer circle, looking at the external and internal food pantry.

And it is making spiritual practice a non-negotiable… the utmost top priority.

Abundant creativity. Passionate drive, A curious spirit. Resilience. And true strength and the COURAGE to allowing ourselves to be seen, heard, and understood… unapologetically STRIPPED NAKED … surrendering to God's plan. TRUST in his plan.

Today I know this as a woman of power.

For me, this is a woman of wealth.

FEMININE PROSPERITY PRACTICE

Wealth and prosperity are much more than money as we identify with it. It is an energy of receptivity, of allowing as well as releasing and circulating. Your inner riches are your true wealth.

Here's a practice designed to support you in opening channels of receptivity:

Declare spiritual practice as your TOP priority. Gratitude. Cultivating Faith. Also, establishing a practice of meditation, prayer, silence, and inner listening will fill your spiritual bank account with clarity and space to receive visions, ideas, opportunities, manifestations of what your heart and soul truly desire.

Take yourself on a SELF-DATE and get radically honest with yourself. Take a holistic wealth assessment, look at every area of your life and rate every 'garden' and learn ways you can flourish in greater receptivity.

The Holistic Wealth Assessment is available at: d.delucainternaitonal@gmail.com

About Donata De Luca

Donata De Luca is a Holistic Wealth Coach who supports high achievers with intuitive guidance and clarifying practices to prevent and heal from burnout and unhealthy 'hustle culture' habits so they can live their truth and expand to stand in their true power.

She is a multi-published author, real estate investor, and founder of *Be the Change Global* for youth... a single mother of young adults and grandmother of twins.

Divine Insight

"If they can't handle your shine,
tell 'em to put on some shades and Shine on Sis!"

Dorothy-Inez Deltufo

From my earliest memories, I've proudly embraced my role as the unique one in my family. I come from a lineage that may not place a high premium on creativity and spirituality, but guess what? Those are the very fibers of my being.

I can vividly recall being just four years old, already singing, dancing, and posing deep, unanswerable questions like, *"If God made me, then who made God?"* It was a question that tickled my curiosity and ignited a lifelong quest for truth and understanding.

Our inner gifts and callings often make their grand entrance during our formative years. But all too often, our well-intentioned loved ones unintentionally snuff out those sparks, believing they know what's best for us. Consequently, we find ourselves living lives and chasing careers that fail to set our souls on fire. We gradually dim our inner light and lose sight of our capacity to shine.

It wasn't until I embarked on my own journey of self-discovery that I found the courage to embrace the radiance of my own star. I let go of the incessant need for external validation, especially from my father, the man I never wanted to disappoint.

As I deepened my spiritual connection, I began to realize that I had a divine purpose, and there were women whose lives I was destined to touch. I began to embody the truth of the Christ consciousness within me, wrapping myself in this newfound authenticity like a warm, comforting blanket. And as I did, my light grew brighter, more radiant, and more magnificent than I could have ever imagined.

Fast forward, my coaching practice blossomed, speaking invitations poured in, I authored books, and, most importantly, I experienced an enduring joy because I was living and breathing as my authentic self.

It's time for you to ponder: *What unique skills, gifts, and talents lie dormant within you, just waiting to be awakened? What yearns to be expressed through the canvas of your life?* Remember, you are not here by chance; you are here on a divine assignment.

As long as you breathe, you have the power to pivot. You don't have to make a grand transformation overnight, but you can take that first courageous step today. Don't leave this world with the haunting question of what your life could have been "if only."

Seek the support you need to take bold action, and on the other side, you will find growth, fulfillment, and boundless joy.

Embrace your light, and Shine on Sis!

FEMININE PROSPERITY PRACTICE

Every morning sit up and begin with three deep, rejuvenating breaths. As you breathe, allow yourself to envision, feel and connect with the inner version of yourself you aspire to become. This empowered woman already resides within you.

Take note of her graceful stride, her confident speech, her insightful thoughts, and her stylish attire. Consider how this version of you prioritizes her day and what deliberate actions she would take to move closer to her dreams today. Then imagine adorning yourself with her essence as if it were a garment.

Look into the mirror of your mind, smile, and shine on Sis!

About Dorothy-Inez Deltufo

Meet Dorothy-Inez Deltufo, the "Queen of Shine"! A three-time International Best-selling Author, Speaker, Holistic Confidence and Self Love Coach.

She's the visionary behind the Shine Collective & Sanctuary for Women, where high-achieving, heart-centered professional women discover their inner radiance through self-love and inner healing.

Connect with Dorothy-Inez:
www.dorothyinez.com

Divine Insight

It is said, beauty is in the eye of the beholder.
Be the beholder.
For it is in that moment the
universe mirrors back
to us our own beautiful soul.

Ella Nebeker

My belief is we choose our legacy by excavating the seeds that were planted within us from the beginning of time. By putting our focus on seeing the beauty in others, nature and things in the material world we find our own perspective of life. Each perspective is unique like our fingerprints, no two are alike.

Take a walk on the wild side with me, meaning nature, of course.

Imagine yourself in a canoe gently floating down the Snake River in Wyoming. Notice the crystal-clear water and the smooth rocks that glimmer under the rays of golden light in the rippling water. The tall pines along the banks are a backdrop to the willows that sway back and forth in the wind.

Do you see the beauty in each of these things?

This is being the beholder, a practice worth implementing into one's life. This is living in the present moment, seeing with gratitude through the eyes of God.

Wait! The water is getting faster, and the rapids are approaching, you must navigate the foamy waters between large bodies of sharp rocks and fallen logs. It's exciting and frightful all at the same time.

Can you still see the beauty?

Suddenly your canoe begins to swamp as you approach another rapid and then the vessel cannot take on anymore of the river and it tips over in the raging rapids. Trying with all of your might to hold on, the canoe drags you along the bottom of the river, your legs are beaten against those smooth rocks that looked so lovely earlier in the day. It may take a little more to behold the beauty when exhaustion, fear and pain from the journey sets in.

Just as the rapids disperse and the river becomes a calm and peaceful you take a deep breath then exhale reflecting upon the fear and adrenaline that consumed you on this tumultuous ride, this too is beauty to behold.

When we choose to see and acknowledge the beauty in all our experiences, our lives change. Sometimes the clarity of the beauty comes a bit later.

Here's one of my own examples; In my 20's after having been married for 3 years I began to suspect infertility problems. I was consumed with having a baby and it wasn't happening. I consulted my OBGYN, had a few invasive tests and month after month I was disappointed and at times devastated.

One day while chatting on the phone with my mom, she mentioned friends of theirs who had a granddaughter that was only 18 months old. Her mother was in prison, the grandparents had custody and were thinking of putting her up for adoption so she could be raised by loving parents. They put us in touch with the attorney and we began preparations. I was riding high on life when I received a call from the attorney telling us that the mother had made threats against us, and it wouldn't be a good idea to proceed with the adoption. Sadness doesn't begin to explain my feelings as I went around returning all the clothes and furniture I had purchased, sobbing in every store. It was though something had died inside me. My dream had died, or so I thought. Two weeks later the same attorney called and said they had a baby boy who hadn't' been born yet and would we be interested in adopting him? Well, hello! Of course, we would! He was born a month early, a five lb. bundle of joy. He gave me the greatest gift, becoming a mom.

Ah, but the story doesn't end there…This baby not only changed my world, he changed my family for generations before and for generations to come. You see he is biracial. We were pioneers in 1986, the first in our families, friends, and congregation to have a biracial child. My parent's generational beliefs of learned racism began to fall away as they fell madly in love with him. Anyone who meets him is charmed by his loving heart, his huge brown eyes, long lashes, and his smile.

Looking back there is so much beauty in our story. There are no real mistakes. Ending the generational racism begins in our homes and then heals our communities, our country, and our world. This was one of my seeds in my Legacy. We are all intertwined in this beautiful tapestry called life.

FEMININE PROSPERITY PRACTICE

Be the beholder, it has made all the difference for me. As my legacy I leave this gift with my children and others it may inspire; always see the beauty, sometimes it's in the moment and sometimes it's in hindsight. It's never too late to see the beauty in God's big picture. Here's to open eyes and open hearts. Cheers.

About Ella Nebeker

A lover of beauty and a seeker of Truth, Ella Nebeker invites you to join her in this journey of aging into the beauty of who you really are.

As an Interior Designer, author, speaker and silver-haired model, she inspires people to embrace life in every decade.

She is married to her soul mate, together they have 8 fabulous grown children and 13 beautiful grandchildren. She currently lives in Salt Lake City, Utah.

For more information about Pamela (Ella) Nebeker and her work visit: PamelaNebeker.com

Divine Insight

When we are authentic in who we are,
we cannot help but illuminate ourselves from the inside out.
So, allow yourself to show that glory to the world.
Because when you do you are more than simply visible,
you are radiant!

Emily Katz

Why do we find it difficult to embrace our own beauty?

When someone compliments you, do you immediately think... oh, it's this dress, or maybe my lipstick? Never imagining, I AM SHINING.

Dismissing a compliment is to deny a part of ourselves.

Most of my life's work has been devoted to enhancing the natural beauty of people who are starring in television and film. While the work I do appears to focus on the outer realm... makeup, beauty, wardrobe, personal image... there is another aspect of my work that's too often overlooked... connecting people with their inner-beauty...enhancing their true essence...capturing their inner radiance... embracing their one-of-a-kind beauty.

When we are authentic in who we are.
We cannot help but illuminate ourselves from the inside out.
To me, this is the definition of true beauty.

At a certain point, I recognized the bloom of youth begins to fade. Sadly, and too often, we begin to become invisible to much of the world. Predominant in the Western Society, younger appears better... translating into an aberration of "*we need to appear young no matter our age.*"

I began to ask myself:

How can I not only help myself but serve others to recognize their inherent value and the magnificence of their beingness in a genuine, authentic way?

It became my goal to support women in doing so. Putting to use the deep skillset I've gained with makeup, beauty, and image I found this is where I can serve in the most meaningful way. It became my mission to move women to embrace who they are at any age.

It's crucial to stay relevant and modern to successfully interface today's world.

Embrace WHO YOU KNOW YOU ARE
and stand in your inner beauty.
We are all worth seeing and have so much to contribute.

Doing the work and diving deep into my own inner consciousness has been instrumental in recognizing my own worth and value as a person. By effect, this translated into the compassionate awareness of another and recognition of their beauty.

What I found is that when we release the against-ness we hold within ourselves ... when we let go of the stories and limiting beliefs that hold us captive... we free up so much energy. As that energy releases, our acceptance of ourselves with all our beauty and flaws allows us to embrace others on their journey.

We all tell ourselves stories.
Some of those stories are embraced as our truths.
Digging down to the reality of who we truly are...
beyond the beliefs and the stories...
takes courage, and a lot of work.

I am still a work in progress. Allowing myself the space for a joyful discovery. Stepping beyond the negative self-talk filled with opinion takes reflective work.

How do we find the path through all that?

It takes patience, gentle self-care, self-love. Meditating has become my haven of transformation at a core level … a transformation that now allows me to express and see the truth of my own inner beauty, embrace it, and shine forth in magnificence while supporting others to do the same.

One of my favorite quotes is from the Dalai Lama:

> *"Be Kind Whenever possible. It is always possible."*
> *Let go of the judgment and begin to be kind, truly kind to yourself.*
> *And remember, as the Dalai Lama says: It's always possible.*

FEMININE PROSPERITY PRACTICE

It's surprising how powerful your morning routine can be.

Try this: As you dress and apply your make-up speak affirmative words.

I embrace my inner beauty and allow it to shine forth.

I make a difference in the world.

I am a beautiful soul expressing my inner beauty to the world.

I stand in my inner-beauty.

I am worthy of being seen and have so much to contribute.

Select and repeat whatever words speak to you.

Use the words to affirm a message you find is true for you.

Notice the radiant different bringing affirmations to your morning routine can make.

About Emily Katz

"It's through an amalgam of experiences that I truly see the beauty in everyone. I'm able to support women to stand in the glory of who they truly are as a magnificent soul."

As an Award-Winning Make-Up Artist/ Image Design, Emily Katz is dedicated to serving and supporting women to solidly stand in their beauty, wisdom, talent, and power of knowing who she is, always investigating how to approach life.

Elle Magazine named Emily Katz awarding her their prestigious *"Beauty Genius" Award*, calling her a Force of Nature. She has worked on critically acclaimed shows such as LOST and 24. Emily works with leading ladies like Sharon Stone, Minnie Driver, Evangeline Lilly, Andie MacDowell, and high-profile actors like Robert Redford, Martin Sheen, Bradley Cooper, Charleton Heston, and James Coburn to name just some of her roster.

For more information about Emily Katz and her work visit: https://ektruth.com

Divine Insight

*Acknowledging the divine energy within us is free and freeing.
It is surprisingly courageous to choose kindness
and compassion for ourselves.*

Lynn Raynr

"I am grateful for myself. And I am enjoying life as I am." These words spoken by my son Eli Raynr, gave me reason to pause. I couldn't help but wonder why I would ever doubt myself… or judge my life… even for one moment longer.

My son Eli constantly impacts people with a tangible omnipresent love. Every day of my life, he says, *"I love you so much, and I'm going to have a great day!"* He has Down Syndrome, and I believe he is my greatest teacher.

Here's the uncomfortable truth: When invited to write about myself as an amazing woman, I thought it somewhat hilarious. I mean really? Even though I have many accomplishments, I still had no idea how my 5'5" frame registered 196 pounds. I had tried most weight loss attempts with scattered success. Deep down I knew my body weight was a spiritual issue. *What was my fat trying to tell me? What was I missing?* Clueless, I prayed. "God, I don't know how to lose weight!" I actually could have substituted the words, *"I don't know how to love myself."*

Moments after my appeal to God, I heard from within, "Lynn, what if instead of wasting time and money in always trying to fix yourself, you had concentrated on your gifts and talents to create a life you love?"

That was a stomach punch realization. What have I done with my life and is it too late?

What if God is real and wants us to be happy?

Let me tell you a story. It's a story that brought me to a new perspective, a new understanding about the importance of love.

Nearly five decades ago during my Spring Break, I answered the phone. I sank to my knees as I was told my 15-year-old brother was dead from a motorcycle accident. Stevie and I were close.

"Please just let me know you're alright," I cried as I went to sleep that night. Imagine my surprise, when he held my hand, sending a euphoric energy throughout my body. He was in a higher place and filled with so much light. *How could I possibly be sad?*

"Oh my God, I thought. *"If we really don't die, then why are we here?"*

Loud and clear I heard from within…

We are here to love.

It is so easy to love others, but how is that possible if we don't love ourselves? I think a lot of people have had childhood traumas. I certainly did, and being sexually abused at five years old, the lens in which I viewed life was askew. I didn't know how to really accept and love myself, even though, in all honesty, I had learned to put on a pretty good act.

A dear friend of mine once said,

> **You have to take care of yourself,**
> **before you can take care of others.**

Bottom line is this, we are all iconic, each given our unique purpose to explore and share with others. It takes courage to release the illusions that keep us trapped in old paradigms, especially with self-judgment. Explore the possibilities.

FEMININE PROSPERITY PRACTICE

Ask yourself, "What if I am loved?"

What if the tapestry of my life has made me who I am, and I am stronger for it?

Close your eyes and be still. Visualize an effervescent white light surrounding yourself. See any judgment or self-doubt releasing as ball of tangled string into the nothingness from which it came. Now jump for joy with gratitude as you embrace your true essence NOW!

Daily mantra:

I AM GRATEFUL FOR MYSELF AND I AM ENJOYING LIFE AS I AM.

About Lynn Raynr

Lynn Raynr is an entrepreneur, writer and producer. She continues to study spirituality and personal development.

Growing up in Alaska, she is also a former broadcast journalist and public relations specialist. Raising her son with Down Syndrome she has learned firsthand the importance of letting love lead and encourages parents, and especially mothers, to practice self-care. *"My goal is to live fully with compassion, humor, and self-expression while inspiring others to do the same."*

Currently living in Carlsbad, California, she is married to her loving husband David, and they have four amazing children.

For more information or to connect with Lynn, you may visit her at: whatifyouareawesome.com
or email at 1balancedwoman@gmail.com

Divine Insight

"I am an artist, a solutionist, and an entrepreneur.
It's not what we do or when we do it,
it's who we are while we're doing it.
If we cannot be ourselves then who will we be?"

Stephanie Graziano

When I was young, I felt silenced, oppressed, always needing to be quiet, staying out of the conversation, being politely unseen. I was raised by a single mother, the oldest of my generation in my father's Asian family. This position held a lot of expectations, from both my mother (struggling to get by) and my father (who had a cultural expectation of his firstborn). The expectations were both stated and inferred. It was a heavy lift for a young girl. No voice, unseen, no roots, struggling to find my way.

It wasn't until I was in my 20's that I began to understand what a gift my youth was. I had learned to watch and to listen, to see and to hear things that others could not. I learned about the consequences of letting others steer your ship and how not speaking up meant just giving in. Then, I learned that I had a voice, that I had control over my choices, that I was a unique individual. So, what did this mean? How could exploring this deeper change the trajectory of what could have been a meek and unfulfilled future?

In my 30's I began to see that I had power. Power to make a difference, to stand up for others, to decide how I wanted to contribute to the world. I began to grab onto my independence. Why not? What's the risk?

In my 40's I understood how to maneuver through the roles of leader, business owner, partner, and parent all at the same time. But how? By being my unique self, detail oriented, sensitive and concerned, organized, and very self-aware. Isn't this when our confidence kicks in?

In my 50's I became aware of my soul journey, the one that no one else will ever experience, it's ours alone. What a fabulous place to be. This is when I decided to explore who I was even more intimately. Who I was — *by nature, by nurture, by choice*. What was it about the lived-life discovery that made me unique?

In my 60's, having been designing my life with more insight and information, I now live in appreciation, gratitude, and love for the miracles experienced every day. I don't have any questions about why my life took the road it did. I know when an opportunity is just right for me or something to let go of.

Notice I have not mentioned anything about work or industry, nor about accomplishments or failures, or titles or accolades, or even family. That's not what it's about. It's not about being anything but yourself. About living in the grace of who you really are.

The awakening of our own unique amazing womanhood is imperative. We will each travel our own timeline. Who we choose to be or become can happen at any age. This was my journey, what does yours look like?

FEMININE PROSPERITY PRACTICE

This practice truly helped me identify the highest level of unique qualities in me. Having this information has helped me make quick decisions, choose the right opportunities, live at my highest level. I would love for you to do the same.

- By Nature – your way of being that is undeniable – for me, I call it **Artist**
- By Nurture – what emerged in you as a result of your upbringing? For me I call it **Solutionist**
- By Choice – How do I choose to move through my journey? For me I call it **Entrepreneur**

Understanding these three qualities of being allows me to make decisions and choices that keep me in a flow state. I feel at ease, creative, rooted, inspired, and so much more.

About Stephanie Graziano

As a 30-year Executive in the Entertainment and Media industries, Stephanie Graziano is passionate about helping entrepreneurs and visionaries create ease in executing their big ideas.

A passionate creative executive, visionary thinker, and results driven strategist, she is a Certified Business Coach (CTACC), certified One Page Planner, and creator of *The Foundation Formula*, an online course for entrepreneur's looking to deepen the Who, What, and How of their business.

A multi-published author, including contributions to *Conscious Entrepreneurs*, a Silver Nautilus Award winning book with Christine Kloser, and *Writer to Writer* with Judith Cassis. Has been profiled in The Hollywood Reporter, The LA Times Business section, The LA Business Journal and Start-Ups magazine.

www.StephanieGraziano.com
www.linkedin.com/in/stephanie-graziano-9603145
www.facebook.com/stephanie.graziano.10/

Activate Your Feminine Prosperity

When one woman stretches her creative desires,
another finds the courage to do the same.

When one woman moves from the sidelines
to speak her truth,
another gives voice to her own.

When one woman stays true to sacred confidence,
another finds the determination to break free of
stress and struggle replacing it with trust and devotion.

In essence,
it begins with one woman,
one woman who activates feminine prosperity.
Maybe that one woman is you.

The dawn of a radiant evolution is upon us.
It's being led by women just like you —
the woman who knows her greatest power to
create goes well beyond day-to-day pushing for results —
she knows true sacred power enlivens her creativity,
ignites infinite potentials and sets her soul on fire!

ACTIVATE YOUR FEMININE PROSPERITY

Write Your Feminine Prosperity Statement

When writing your FEMININE PROSPERITY Statement, there are two different perspectives you can consider.

The first viewpoint is to write a FEMININE PROSPERITY Statement as one that is written to yourself. Here you can consider it as a declarative statement, a SACRED AGREEMENT to which you promise to hold yourself accountable. In this instance, the statement is one directed towards being, creating, becoming, and embracing the wealth of your feminine prosperity.

The second perspective of writing a FEMININE PROSPERITY Statement is one that is written to inspire others. Again, it is a declarative affirmation. It reflects an aspect of FEMININE PROSPERITY you wish to inspire others to embrace or to amplify in our feminine consciousness.

Here are a few clarifying questions to support you in writing your FEMININE PROSPERITY statement:

- What feminine value do you wish to magnify within yourself or others?
- What sacred power do you wish to affirm?
- What strengths and creative capacities do you wish to encourage and elevate?
- What aspect of feminine prosperity do you wish to create more of in your life, or in your community, or in the world?

A final note before you begin to write your FEMININE PROSPERITY Statement: Avoid using statements such as, *"I will be"* or *"I wish to be"* or any other derivatives of these types of statements, as they are a confirmation of lack. The fact is you are already equipped with a wealth of feminine prosperity. So, you can consider the FEMININE PROSPERITY Statement as an activating statement for recognizing, remembering, and affirming.

Here are a few examples of topics to consider when writing your FEMININE PROSPERITY Statement:

- I allow my intuitive giftedness to magnify opportunities.
- I elevate my worth and honor my worthiness.
- I amplify my authentic voice.
- I practice radical receptivity and allow greater creative ease.
- I trust and know I am here to make a difference.
- I rise in the feminine way of success and achievement.
- I pause and align with the radiant rhythm of my soul.
- I expand a richness of awareness in every experience.

Here are a few FEMININE PROSPERITY values you may also wish to consider when writing your statement.

- ➢ Connectedness. Wholeheartedness.
- ➢ Humility, listening, learning from others.

- ➢ Sincerity, a willingness to speak openly and honestly.
- ➢ Patience, a recognition that some solutions emerge slowly.
- ➢ Empathy, sensitivity to others that promotes understanding.
- ➢ Trustworthiness, strength that inspires confidence.
- ➢ Openness, receptivity.
- ➢ Flexibility, the ability to change and adapt when circumstances require.
- ➢ Vulnerability, bold courage, trust in the unknown.
- ➢ Meaning, sense of purpose.
- ➢ Being articulate, expressing clearly, heart centered.
- ➢ Being dependable, impeccability of our word.
- ➢ Collaboration, flexibility, and cooperation.

A few additional include:

- ➢ Intuition
- ➢ Sensuality
- ➢ Self-love
- ➢ Self-care
- ➢ Kindness, compassion
- ➢ Generosity, giving
- ➢ Honesty, sincerity
- ➢ Nurturance, caring

I Embrace the Wealth of Feminine Prosperity

Signature _____

Date: _____

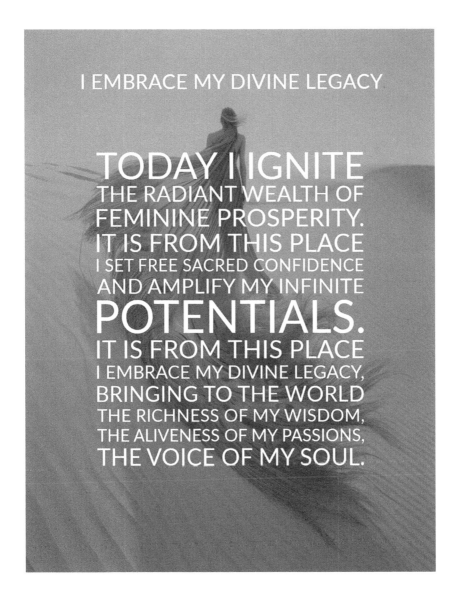

I EMBRACE MY DIVINE LEGACY.

TODAY I IGNITE
THE RADIANT WEALTH OF
FEMININE PROSPERITY.
IT IS FROM THIS PLACE
I SET FREE SACRED CONFIDENCE
AND AMPLIFY MY INFINITE
POTENTIALS.
IT IS FROM THIS PLACE
I EMBRACE MY DIVINE LEGACY,
BRINGING TO THE WORLD
THE RICHNESS OF MY WISDOM,
THE ALIVENESS OF MY PASSIONS,
THE VOICE OF MY SOUL.

Amazing
Woman
Nation

Amazing Woman Nation

WE BELIEVE THE CREATIVITY OF WOMEN CAN AND WILL TRANSFORM THE WORLD!

Amazing Woman Nation is dedicated to evolving the culture of women's success. Founded by Marsh Engle, the movement is dedicated to elevating every woman's sense of purpose and creativity by curating a collection of educational programs, published books, engaging events, and social impact campaigns positioned to move millions.

Since 2001 AMAZING WOMAN books, training programs, podcasts, and events have been recognized for their unparalleled capacity to move women to develop herself as an entrepreneurial leader, launch mission-driven businesses, and create greater impact in the world.

The AMAZING WOMAN NATION philanthropic initiative joins women in a collective intention to create a more empowered future for the next generation of amazing women. Together we aspire to create a world that fully harnesses the power of women to create lasting and positive change in their own lives, in their communities, and in the world.

Philanthropic contributions have supported leading organizations, including YWCA, DARE (Drug Abuse Resistance Education), RAINN (Rape, Abuse, Incest National Network), National Center for Missing & Exploited Children, CAREorg, YWCA (Eliminating Racism. Empowering Women), Dress for Success (Empowering women to achieve economic independence) and Safe Passage.

If you would like to learn more about THE AMAZING WOMAN NATION podcasts, courses, and events visit:

www.AmazingWomanNation.com

Join us on FACEBOOK
https://www.facebook.com/AMAZINGWOMANNATION/

Acknowledgments

Thank you to every woman who believes in the vision of this book. Your sheer commitment to bring your energy, inspiration, words and wisdom to the page moves me to continuously reach higher.

Thank you to my mother and my grandmother for urging me forward in the *search for the amazing woman* leading to my life's work.

Always and forever, love goes to my two sons — Jason and Jon — to my beautiful daughters-in-law, Czerny and Hanae. And to my two grandsons, Jacky and Rio.

Thank you to the thousands of women who have attended *Amazing Woman Live events,* purchased AMAZING WOMAN books and have taken part in AMAZING WOMAN programs — from Maui to Montreal, Los Angeles to Toronto — your commitment to become the amazing woman you are called to become is at the very foundation of the AMAZING WOMAN MOVEMENT.

To the hundreds of clients, past and present, whose purpose and vision are steeped in the wealth of feminine prosperity. It has been my sincere privilege to support you in some way to embrace your most worthy mission.

To my readers and friends who connect with me on my Facebook pages, INSTAGRAM, and LinkedIn. Thank you for the continuous words of encouragement or for simply stopping by to say hello. I love our connection.

I hold great respect for the countless thought leaders and authors, who continue to stir my curiosity, broaden my perspective, and deepen my spiritual connection. Thank you.

To my valued spiritual mentors, colleagues, business consultants, mastermind partners, publisher, and agents… you are forever valued and appreciated.

And, to my cherished friends, thank you for bringing so much inspiration, love, and sheer joy into my life. Your stream of encouragement never fails to move me. And your friendship touches my heart beyond words.

About Marsh Engle

Marsh Engle is dedicated to evolving the culture of women's success. Her multi-decade work trailblazes practices that lead women to find and flourish in an unshakeable confidence, reclaiming their voices, and acting upon their highest potentials. Creator of the bestselling AMAZING WOMAN co-authored book series and founder of THE AMAZING WOMAN NATION, her training programs and events are recognized for their unparalleled capacity to move women to define, communicate and realize the radiant wealth of feminine prosperity.

In 2016, Marsh served as an elected delegate to THE UNITED STATE OF WOMEN, an acclaimed leadership program led by First Lady Michelle Obama. She's received awards from the Congress of the United States and the City of Los Angeles for her work to elevate women's entrepreneurial leadership. Marsh has shared the stage with bestselling authors including don Miguel Ruiz and Marianne Williamson and acclaimed Journalists Maria Shriver.

Since 1999 her philanthropic contributions have supported leading cause-driven organizations including, DARE (Drug Abuse Resistance

Education), RAINN (Rape, Abuse, Incest National Network), Susan G. Komen Breast Cancer Foundation, National Center for Missing & Exploited Children, CARE, YWCA (Eliminating Racism. Empowering Women), Dress for Success (Empowering women to achieve economic independence) and Safe Passage.

For more information about Marsh Engle visit:
www.MarshEngle.com

Connect with Marsh on Facebook:
https://www.facebook.com/marsh.engle/
https://www.facebook.com/OFFICIALMarshEngle/

Connect with Marsh on LinkedIn:
https://www.linkedin.com/in/marshengle

Connect with Marsh on Instagram:
https://www.instagram.com/marshengle/

A REVOLUTIONIZING 21-DAY
SPIRITUAL WRITING PRACTICE
FREE EBOOK BONUS | DOWNLOAD NOW
*A spiritual woman's guide to activating the
radiant wealth of her feminine prosperity*

- Easy-to-follow writing prompts to support you in activating SPIRITUAL CONFIDENCE and tap into THE RADIANT WEALTH OF YOUR FEMININE PROSPERITY.
- A SACRED BREATH MEDITATION PRACTICE energizes intentions and activates feminine actions.
- A collection of SACRED AGREEMENTS awakens a new level of alignment with your purpose, authentic communication, and fulfillment of your true callings.

*Imagine those purposeful potentials you've yet to access…
the wisdom you've yet to give voice…
the passions you've yet to unleash.*

Download your FREE eBook now.

**You are invited to join a twice-per-month
Mentorship Mastermind for entrepreneurial women
who have a brilliant calling in their heart and
are ready to liberate the radiant wealth of their work.**

*We gather to elevate the wealth of our work.
The power of community.
The alignment of soul, message and legacy.
The energetics of stunning success.*

More bestselling co-authored books written and compiled by Marsh Engle

https://amzn.to/47SmMzP   https://amzn.to/494HFsz   https://amzn.to/3HxlQpL

The creativity of Amazing Women is transforming the world
– helping to make lives richer, better, and more meaningful.
Each in the series of Amazing Woman co-authored books is
designed to magnify your unique and individual giftedness
and communicate in ways that amplifies you true expression,
gives deeper meaning to your purpose,
and brings significance to your sacred work.

For more information about the Amazing Woman multi-book
co-authored series visit: www.AmazingWomanNation.com

Made in United States
Cleveland, OH
13 February 2025

14210554R00134